KURSK

THE GREATEST TANK BATTLE

1943

KURSK

THE GREATEST TANK BATTLE
1943

M. K. BARBIER

Ian Allan
PUBLISHING

First published 2002

ISBN 0 7110 2868 0

Copyright © 2002 Amber Books Ltd

Published by Ian Allan Publishing
an imprint of Ian Allan Publishing Ltd, Hersham, Surrey KT12 4RG.

Code: 0204/B

Editorial and design by
Amber Books Ltd
Bradley's Close
74-77 White Lion Street
London N1 9PF

Project Editor: Charles Catton
Design: www.stylus-design.com
Picture Research: Lisa Wren
Maps by Patrick Mulrey

Picture credits:
Ian Baxter/History in the Making: 33, 34, 35 (b), 36, 37, 38, 39, 58, 59, 60 (both), 61, 62, 64, 65 (both), 66 (both), 69 (t), 70, 71, 76, 77, 78 (t), 79, 81, 82, 86 (t), 88-89, 90, 91, 95, 97, 98 (both), 100 (both), 101, 103 (b), 104, 105, 108, 109, 113 (t), 115 (both), 116, 120, 124, 126, 127, 129, 131, 133 (t), 134 (both), 135, 136, 139. Süddeutscher Verlag: 6-7, 8, 10, 11, 12, 13, 14, 15, 16, 20 (t),.21, 22, 24-25, 27, 28, 29 (t), 30, 31, 35 (t),56-57, 75, 99, 125, 132. Novosti: 20 (b), 23, 54 (both), 83 (t), 121, 122-123, 130, 137. POPPERFOTO: 26 (both), 40-41, 42, 43, 45, 46 (b), 47, 48, 49. TRH Pictures: 9 (USNA), 17, 18, 19, 32, 51 (both), 53 (b), 63, 68, 72-73, 74, 78 (b), (USNA), 85, 87, 92, 93, 94, 96, 102, 110, 111, 113 (b) (USNA), 117, 118, 119, 133 (b), 138 (b), 141. Ukrainian Central State Archive of Cine-Photo Documents: 29 (b), 44, 46 (t), 50, 52, 53 (t), 58 (b), 69 (b), 83 (t), 84, 86 (b), 103 (t), 106-107, 112, 128, 138 (t), 140.

Printed and bound in Italy by: Eurolitho S.p.A., Cesano Boscone (MI)

Contents

The Eastern Front

June 1941 – January 1943

The titanic clash that was the battle of Kursk was the culmination of two years of vicious, hard-fought combat between the two polar opposites of Hitler's Nazi Germany and Stalin's Communist Soviet Union.

Although Hitler may have had much cause for concern after Germany's horrific defeat at Stalingrad, he was by no means ready to give up his struggle against the Soviet Union. After all, the defeat of communism and the supposedly subhuman Slavic peoples of the Soviet Union had always been a central goal of Nazi ideology. Hitler had, moreover, faced considerable adversity in the past, but in the end he had always triumphed over any difficulties. As a young man, he had been wounded during Germany's ill-fated attempt to defeat the Allies in World War I; in the political sphere, his first major offensive – the so-called Beer Hall Putsch of 1923 in Munich – had ended with a jail sentence. Now, two decades later, Hitler faced bleak prospects once again. Furthermore, the magnitude of the disaster at Stalingrad, where what was left of the encircled German 6th Army surrendered to the Soviet Red Army on 2 February 1943, was, of course, far greater than the setback he had suffered years earlier in his attempt to seize power in Munich.

Still, Hitler refused to believe that all was lost, and he took comfort in the way German forces under the direction of Field Marshal Erich von Manstein had regained

Left: The early months of the war in the East did not go well for the Soviet Union. Here Soviet soldiers of the Red Army surrender to a German armoured column on the plains of Russia.

Left: For Adolf Hitler, the Führer of the Third Reich, the German invasion of the Soviet Union was nothing less than a crusade against the perceived evils of communism and the Slavic peoples of the East.

much lost territory in the wake of the surrender at Stalingrad. In fact, by June of 1943, he found himself confronted with a very tempting strategic opportunity: a great bulge in the enemy lines centred on Kursk, a town best known before the war for its destruction at the hands of Mongols in 1240, and for the iron-ore deposits below its soil that rendered compasses useless.

Within the huge salient, measuring 190km (120 miles) wide by 120km (75 miles) deep, were troops of the Soviet Central and Voronezh fronts (army groups). If the German forces could attack from the north and the south in a huge pincer movement, it would be possible for them to encircle the Soviets. They could then destroy them in a bloody *Kesselschlacht*, or 'cauldron battle', of the kind the Germans had used to amass unprecedented tactical victories during the first part of the war against the Soviets. The Germans would thereby not only succeed in regaining territory and annihilating countless

Left: For Adolf Hitler, the Führer of the Third Reich, the German invasion of the Soviet Union was nothing less than a crusade against the perceived evils of communism and the Slavic peoples of the East.

Soviet forces, but would also improve Germany's international position.

In Hitler's view, Kursk would 'light a bonfire' that would impress the world. Such an impression was especially important from a diplomatic perspective. In addition to the well-publicised awful defeat the Germans had suffered at Stalingrad, they had also lost North Africa to the Allies between 1942 and 1943. As a result, representatives of the Italian and Romanian governments had begun to make discreet inquiries about some sort of peace agreement. Turkey had finally made the decision not to act against the Soviet Union in the Caucasus, and German foreign minister Joachim von Ribbentrop had even found it necessary to warn the Finnish Government against seeking to come to terms with the Soviets.

On top of these diplomatic motives, strategic concerns also provided some of the impetus for Germany to preserve the initiative it had regained on the Eastern Front with Manstein's counter-offensive at Kharkov. Although Hitler and his generals realised that their strategic goal now had to be far more limited than it had been at the onset of the German–Soviet war in 1941, they nonetheless believed that a successful attack at Kursk would have value. Such an offensive, code-named Operation Citadel, would inflict enough damage on the Red Army to keep it from launching its own major attack, while at the same time giving the German forces the chance to consolidate their defences. It was meant to be the most significant of several other limited offensives aimed at this same general goal.

Not surprisingly, the enormous salient at Kursk also attracted much attention from the Soviet dictator Joseph Stalin, who recognised not only its vulnerability, but also its potential as a starting point for future offensives to the west. Like Hitler, Stalin had a strong interest in military strategy, but by this point he was also learning – unlike the Führer – to allow his generals more leeway in making operational and even strategic decisions. This difference in the abilities of Hitler and Stalin to learn from past mistakes would play a crucial role in the battle of Kursk. Furthermore, in addition to this contrast in personalities at the top, the realities of combat that the armies of both sides had already experienced on the Eastern Front – from generals to common soldiers – would provide the context for Operation Citadel.

The massive clash of armies that had gone on for two years now on the Eastern Front was in its essence the product of the ideology and aspirations of Adolf Hitler. Germany's invasion of the Soviet Union in June 1941, code-named Operation Barbarossa, stemmed from Hitler's desire to attain *Lebensraum*, or 'living space', for his expanding German Reich. Not unlike the way in which the United States had expanded westwards across the vast North American continent in the nineteenth century, and Britain had amassed a great colonial empire, Germany was to realise its own 'manifest destiny' by conquering and settling huge stretches of land to its east. Hitler considered the native Slavic peoples to be racially inferior to German 'Aryans', and he thus had no qualms about forcing them into subservience, or even death, if they stood in the way of Germany's expansion. Of course, anti-Semitism had always been more of a cornerstone of Hitler's ideology than his disdain for Slavs, and Germany's eastern conquests put him in control of Europe's largest populations of Jews, who were located in Poland and western Russia. In effect, then, World War II can be seen not only as a war of conquest, but also as one of extermination in a struggle for racial survival.

In fact, even some German military leaders who otherwise offered no tangible resistance to Hitler's leadership would register protests over the extreme methods of the *SS-Einsatzgruppen*, who uprooted and slaughtered countless civilians in the eastern theatre during the time of German occupation. Aside from any moral objections some German military leaders might have had, they also felt that the harsh policies of the SS were counterproductive. Such policies engendered resistance from people who might otherwise have welcomed German 'liberation' from Stalinist repression, such as the Ukrainians, no lovers of Stalin or the communists, and, in some cases, also diverted resources that might have been of use against the Red Army.

Nevertheless, during the first part of the war in the East, the German military had, in general, performed very well against its Soviet counterpart. On 22 June 1941, German troops crossed the border into the Soviet Union; Operation Barbarossa, which had evolved from a plan outlined by Major General

Marcks almost a year earlier, began. According to Hitler's plan, 120 divisions had less than five months in which to destroy the Soviet Union. The destruction of the Red Army would be accomplished in two phases: a series of *Kesselschlachts* to destroy the Soviet forces in European Russia, followed by a battle of annihilation for Moscow. The annihilation had to be completed before the start of winter, but Hitler was confident that the German Army's tactical excellence made strategic military victory in a single campaign (or *Vernichtungschlacht*) possible. Inherently inferior, the Soviet Army would be unable to mount a defence that could withstand the German assault. The earlier campaigns in Poland and France seemed to support the German strategy; however, when implemented in Operation Barbarossa, a *Vernichtungschlacht* proved just beyond reach.

The German force that rolled into the Soviet Union in June 1941 numbered over three million

Below: Josef Stalin, seen here with Molotov, his Foreign Minister. Despite warnings from the British, Stalin refused to countenance the idea that the Germans would invade the Soviet Union in 1941.

9

men, supported by more than 3000 tanks and assault guns and 2770 aircraft. The three German Army Groups included seven armies and four panzer groups that contained 17 panzer and 13 motorised divisions. More than half a million motorised vehicles and an even greater number of horses supported this huge force. In addition to German troops, the invasion force included Finnish and Romanian divisions. Planning to destroy the Soviet Army in a bloody *Kesselschlacht*, the German armies implemented *Blitzkrieg*, or lightning warfare, which the Wehrmacht had tested in Poland and France. According to the plan, the Luftwaffe would create havoc behind the enemy lines and render the Soviet air force helpless. Armoured and mechanised units would penetrate and encircle the Red Army, which the infantry would then destroy.

Although plagued by problems, the Red Army, because of its vast resources in manpower and

patriotism, did not crumble, as Hitler anticipated it would, when it met the 'superior' German Army in battle. In June 1941, the Germans encountered a Red Army commanded by a leadership still reeling from the purges of the 1930s. Many field commanders and staff officers were inexperienced or incompetent, yet Josef Stalin expected them to do the impossible: stop the German advance. A hero at Stalingrad (or Tsaritsyn as the city was then known) during the civil war, Stalin demanded that his forces defend every inch of the existing frontier. Most officers interpreted this to mean that they could not lose any territory. As a result, they generally distributed the Soviet armies evenly across the front, rather than concentrating them in key areas. Stalin's control over strategic command did not encourage independent initiative by the officers: in fact, it was positively discouraged. Most, therefore, only attempted to apply textbook solutions, even if they were inappropriate in the situation facing them.

The Soviets' military organisation included more than 300 divisions, which exceeded German estimates, but none of the formations was equivalent to

Below: German soldiers fire at their opponents from the cover of a building in late June 1941. The Soviet frontier guards had no warning of the impending attack, and were swept aside by the Wehrmacht.

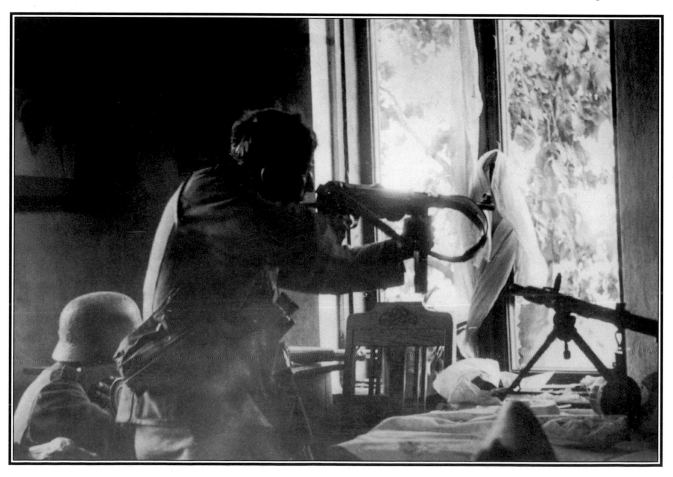

the Panzer Group or the Panzer Army in being able to accomplish large-scale, in-depth penetration of the enemy's rear. The Soviet mechanised divisions were unbalanced and dispersed in a way that made the concentration of these formations difficult. In addition, while the Germans had medium tanks in the field – generally Mark IIIs and Mark IVs – the majority of Soviet tanks were lightly armoured and poorly armed T-26s. By 1941, however, the Red Army had just begun to field new tanks, the T-34 mediums and the KV-1 heavy tanks, both of which surprised the Germans and were effective against their tanks. Unfortunately, most of the Soviet tanks lacked radios, hampering their effective use, and the number of tanks was initially insufficient to meet a strong enemy threat. The Soviets did not fare any better against the Germans in the air. Although Russian aircraft outnumbered those possessed by the Luftwaffe by a significant margin, the Soviet equipment was obsolete and worn out. Consequently, the Soviet air force did little to hinder German dominance of the skies at the beginning of the war.

Although Hitler believed that the Red Army's weaknesses guaranteed a quick victory, German troops faced problems of size and distance on the Eastern Front that were absent in their previous campaigns. The distance across France between the Ardennes Forest and the Atlantic coast was only 322km (200 miles), meaning the German Army could advance so rapidly into enemy territory that the defending army could not fall back and reorganise in the face of the onslaught. The battle for France took six weeks. Although Hitler allotted five months for the destruction of the Soviet Union, the campaign in the East would last much longer. Operation Barbarossa included a three-pronged advance into the Soviet Union: in the north towards Leningrad; in the centre towards Moscow; and in the south towards Rostov and the Caucasus. The distance from the border to Leningrad was more than 800km (500 miles), to Moscow 960km (600 miles) and to Rostov 1440km (900 miles). The length of the German line from the Baltic to the Black Sea was 1280km (795 miles). Therefore, the immediate theatre of operations was more than 960,000 square kilometres (370,660 square miles), which was a great deal of territory, even for three million men, to conquer and occupy. In addition, the farther the German armies advanced into the Soviet Union, the longer and more tenuous their supply lines became. When the war in

Above: A German soldier prepares to throw a stick grenade at an enemy position in the summer of 1941. His colleague crouches, ready to follow up and attack the enemy after the grenade detonates.

the East did not end in five months, the German formations increasingly began to experience logistical problems that neither Hitler nor the German High Command had anticipated. As Hitler did not entertain the notion that Operation Barbarossa could fail or last longer than five months, no contingency plans existed. Consequently, the logistical constraints not only slowed down the German advance, but also became increasingly critical during the Soviet winter of 1941, particularly as the troops of the Wehrmacht had not been issued with winter gear as a result of Hitler's overconfidence.

Operation Barbarossa got off to an auspicious start. The Luftwaffe destroyed 2000 Soviet aircraft on the ground on the first day of the offensive, and the Germans achieved air superiority. Coordinating air and ground attack, the all-arms cooperation worked extremely well within the panzer divisions. The coordination proved less successful in other divisions because the armoured and mechanised formations tended to outdistance the supporting infantry.

Consequently, the infantry frequently bore the brunt of desperate Soviet counter-attacks. Although these tactics had worked well in Poland and France, they did not bring total victory against the Soviets before the onset of winter. However, the slow advance of the infantry formations did not prevent the German armies from advancing 322km (200 miles) in the first five days. The Germans' vast encirclements (*Kesselschlachten*) destroyed 98 Soviet divisions in the first week. On 3 July, German troops encircled Bialystok, where they captured 290,000 Soviets and destroyed 2500 tanks. After surrounding Smolensk,

Left: A Wehrmacht lieutenant (right) and members of his squad on a motorcycle sidecar combination keep an eye out for enemy activity and aircraft. The lieutentant is armed with an MP38 submachine gun.

Below: Weather conditions in Russia were extreme, with baking heat in the summer and freezing cold in the winter. Here a German soldier wipes the sweat off his chin with a cloth.

the Germans took 350,000 prisoners on 15 July. By mid-July, enemy troops were less than 160km (100 miles) from Leningrad and about 322km (200 miles) from Moscow.

Although the armies in the north and centre advanced rapidly, Army Group South (AGS) moved much more slowly. AGS encountered Soviet armoured divisions with T-34 tanks, which could stand up to the German PzKpfw Mark IIIs and IVs. When the severe Soviet resistance held up the German advance outside Kiev, Hitler made a critical strategic error. In September he shifted armour from Army Group Centre (AGC) to the south. Although the additional forces helped surround the 600,000 enemy troops at Kiev, the transfer shifted the momentum of the German advance and prevented the occupation of Moscow on schedule. Soviet forces in the centre had been on the run, and the Germans missed the opportunity to crush them. By relaxing the pressure, the Germans gave the Soviets an opportunity to regroup in the vast Russian hinterland and prepare Moscow's defences.

By 30 September, Operation Barbarossa was basically over. Although the Germans had destroyed approximately 200 Soviet divisions and took more than three million prisoners, they suffered 400,000 casualties, which they could not replace as easily as the Soviets could. Hitler and the German High Command had underestimated their enemy for racial reasons. In addition, they had greatly misjudged the ability of the Soviet Union to raise new forces. The Germans had estimated the existence of 190 Soviet divisions, which was fewer than the actual number of divisions destroyed by the Germans. By September, the Germans had identified 360 enemy divisions on the battlefield. Hitler was not, however, ready to call an end to Barbarossa, and he shifted the focus of the German offensive back to Moscow.

On 2 October 1941, German forces launched a new offensive against the Soviet capital. Operation Typhoon began with great encirclements and tactical victories. Within a week, German forces had encircled the majority of the four Soviet armies west of Viaz'ma, but they had a hard time containing them within the encirclement. Some enemy troops broke free. The Germans did, however, with some help from Soviet soldiers defecting to their side, destroy many enemy heavy weapons and vehicles. Overall, the German offensive went well initially, and the Soviet responses were weak.

Above: The Soviet T-34 was superior to any German tank it faced, but was not available in significant numbers in 1941. It came as a shock to the Germans, who arrogantly expected their tanks to be the best.

The situation began to change, however, when the first snowfall began on the night of 6 October. The snow was followed by the *rasputiza*, or rainy period of mud, which strikes Russia each spring and autumn as the seasons change. The word *rasputiza* literally means 'time without roads', in reference to the periods when travel in the Soviet Union, which had few paved roads, was extremely difficult. As the attackers discovered, they lost mobility until the ground froze solid. The Soviets took advantage of the Germans' loss of momentum and their own experience in coping with the *rasputiza*. Although the Germans threatened Leningrad and Rostov, Stalin ordered Marshal Georgi Zhukov to leave Leningrad and organise the defence of Moscow. Once he reached the city, Zhukov ordered a series of spoiling attacks to divert the Germans, in order to allow his forces time to prepare the defences outside Moscow.

By mid-November, the ground was frozen solid, and Field Marshal Fedor von Bock's AGC resumed the attack. The AGC's supply line became increasingly vulnerable for every 100m (110yd) the force advanced. Despite their tenuous logistics, however, the Germans were only a few kilometres from Moscow by 27 November. The 3rd Tank Group threatened the city from the north and the 4th Tank Group from the south. Because of its limited resources and the terrain, AGC was forced to advance on a narrow front, which exposed its flanks. By the end of November, the Russian winter was in full swing, and the temperature dropped drastically. The lack of adequate antifreeze for the mechanised

formations slowed the advance even more, and it was so cold the oil in the Germans' weapons froze, rendering them useless. The German situation was much worse than Hitler realised.

The Soviets did not stand idly by while the Germans moved towards Moscow. In addition to reinforcing their defences, Zhukov planned a counter-offensive. During the first week of December, the Germans repeatedly tried to regain their momentum. As each attempt failed, troop exhaustion and losses, as well as dwindling supplies, took their toll. Then, on 6 December, Soviet forces under Zhukov's direction launched a massive counter-attack against the overextended, vulnerable AGC. With the situation desperate, Bock, the commander of AGC, requested permission to withdraw. Field Marshal Walter von Brauchitsch, the chief of OKH, and General Franz Halder, the chief of the General Staff, both supported Bock. Hitler denied the request and forced Bock to resign his command. Bock's replacement was the first of many. Between 17 and 25 December, Hitler replaced Brauchitsch; General Heinz Guderian, the commander of the 2nd Panzer Army; General Erich Höppner, the commander of the 4th Panzer Army; and General von Strauss, the commander of the 9th Army. When he removed Brauchitsch as chief of OKH, Hitler himself assumed the role of overall commander of the army.

By the end of December 1941, the German threat to Moscow had basically ended. The Soviet counter-attack continued until the spring of 1942 but Hitler refused to allow the AGC to surrender any territory. The Führer concluded that his 'stand fast' order was responsible for the fact that some of the force survived. Consequently, he would apply the same order a year later at Stalingrad, with much more serious consequences. Contrary to Hitler's conclusions, the German troops around Moscow survived because the Soviets tried to do too much too fast. On 5 January, Stalin, against Zhukov's advice, ordered a general offensive across the entire Eastern Front. The overly ambitious counter-offensive failed to achieve Stalin's objectives, and the Red Army's advance slowed increasingly over the next two months. The pace of the Soviet counter-attack allowed the Germans to begin regrouping by March 1942. Operation Typhoon was not, however, without its costs. Although the Germans succeeded in stabilising the front, they failed to defeat the Soviet Union in one campaign. The German army in the East had suffered more than one million casualties, which reduced it in size to only two-thirds of what it had been in June 1941. Furthermore, in December 1941, Germany acquired a new enemy: the United States. These facts failed to deter the Führer.

Even though the battle for Moscow did not officially end until 20 April 1942, Hitler was already planning the next big German summer offensive. On 5 April, he issued a new directive, Führer Directive 41, which outlined the proposed summer campaign in the Crimea, the Don Steppe and the Caucasus. For a number of reasons, including the spring *rasputiza* (thaw), the Germans would not launch Operation Blau (Blue) until late June 1942. In the meantime, both the Soviets and the Germans utilised the time to rest, regroup and prepare for the summer campaign. Recognising the need for reorganisation, the Stavka (Soviet Supreme Command) issued orders to form 'shock' armies with massed artillery on narrow axes to execute deep offensive breakthroughs and exploitation. General Fedorenko began to rebuild large-scale Soviet armoured forces. The mechanised corps of division size numbered only eight. Between 1943 and 1944, they would increase to six tank armies of 40,000–60,000 men and 600–1000 tanks.

Both the Soviets and the Germans suffered huge losses of men and material during Operation Barbarossa and the Soviet winter counter-offensive. While the Soviet Union had vast resources that it could draw upon to replenish its losses, Germany did not. As a result of the depletion of men and equipment, even with replacements, AGS could function at only 85 per cent of its intended strength. Neither Army Group North (AGN) nor AGC had enough transport to launch a large-scale mobile operation. Although the panzer formations succeeded in regaining much of their combat power, other formations failed to do so.

The losses of 1941 and early 1942 meant that the German forces could not mount another strategic attack along the entire front. Hitler therefore decided to attack in the south in order to accomplish two goals. First, he wanted to seize the important economic resources of the Volga and the Caucasus oilfields. He argued that acquiring these resources was crucial in order for Germany to continue the war.

Below: Although smoke obstructs their view and the dense air makes breathing difficult, a German machine gun team carefully make their way forwards through tall grass during the battles near Kiev in 1941.

Secondly, Hitler planned to inflict a decisive defeat upon the Red Army. The German armies would accomplish in 1942 what they had failed to do in 1941. If Germany was going to win in the East, it had to do so between 1942 and 1943.

Both sides began to prepare for the summer offensives. Evaluating the previous year's campaigns, Stalin concluded that Soviet forces could simply attack the Germans, as they had around Moscow, and they could win. Although he pushed for an attack, Stalin's military advisers urged preparation first. Throughout 1942, Stalin would repeatedly pressure his generals to attack long before they felt ready to do so. The Soviet Union's greatest advantage in the spring of 1942 was its ability to regenerate its forces. The Red Army re-trooped and re-supplied at an extremely fast rate. Although Stalin continued to press the army to launch a 'deep battle' offensive, General Zhukov, whom Stalin had come to trust, emphasised that the Red Army was not yet capable

Below: Although a modern war, both armies still relied upon horse-drawn wagons to transport supplies. An exhausted horse sinks to its knees while trying to pull a heavy wagon through deep mud.

of mounting such an offensive. In addition, Stalin wanted the Soviet Army to launch offensives in three different, unrelated regions: around the Crimea; near Kharkov in the Ukraine, which would protect the route to Stalingrad; and in the far north. Although Zhukov warned him that this would dissipate their forces and leave them unprepared to receive the expected German attack, Stalin would not relent.

Both Stalin and Hitler would make unrealistic demands of their armies. Hitler came away from the 1941–1942 campaign with the idea that his 'stand fast' order had led to success. In addition, he incorrectly assumed that he could use the Luftwaffe to supply his forces on the front. Although Operation Barbarossa demonstrated the weaknesses of their strategic thinking, the Germans failed to change. They still relied on the concept of a decisive battle, of a quick victory in Russia with a knockout blow. At the same time, however, they also recognized the need to cut the Soviets off from their resources in the Caucasus, particularly the oil. The Germans could not, however, accomplish Hitler's goals for 1942 unless the German High Command reorganised and re-supplied the army. Because the supply situation

Above: Russian peasant men and women were pressed into service to dig fortifications, tank traps and other defences in a desperate attempt to stop the German advance on Moscow.

was especially bad in the south, the Germans shifted troops from AGN and AGC to AGS. Despite this large transfer of troops to the south, the AGS still did not reach 100 per cent strength. Furthermore, supplying AGS remained a problem. Although the Germans requisitioned trucks from all over Europe and sent them to the Eastern Front, two-thirds of them broke down before they reached their destination. Consequently, logistical problems continually plagued the Germans.

Once Hitler had decided where he wanted to attack, his staff had to devise a plan. The result was Operation Blau, which included a deception plan. According to the deception, the Germans would threaten another attack on Moscow in order to divert Soviet troops from the south. AGS would then

launch Operation Blau, which would proceed in three phases. During the first phase, German troops were supposed to penetrate Soviet defences around Kursk and conduct a typical encirclement. Before the second phase, Field Marshal von Bock was to split the AGS into two army groups: Army Group A and Army Group B. Army Group A, which would conduct the main drive, would advance directly to the Caucasus and take the oil-rich area. Meanwhile, Army Group B, after crossing the Donetz and Don rivers, would proceed to the River Volga north of Stalingrad, in order to cut Soviet communications

Above: Echoing images from the London Blitz of 1940, inhabitants of Moscow shelter from a German air raid on the city in the Mayakovskaya station of the Metro system in the winter of 1941.

Above: The Eastern Front, showing the extent of the German advance in 1941, the Soviet counterattacks of the winter, and Operation Blue, the German summer offensive of 1942 in the south.

with the Caucasus region. Problems arose because Hitler insisted upon the split of the AGS and two separate advances. Consequently, neither army group was in a position to help the other when they encountered difficulties. Furthermore, the front became bigger and overextended.

The deception plan basically worked. The Soviets naturally believed that German forces would renew the assault against Moscow and Leningrad, with the goal of surrounding and defeating the core of the Red Army. After the new Moscow and Leningrad offensive, the Soviets expected the Germans to initiate an attempt to cut Russia off from its resources in the Caucasus. Stalin concurred with his military advisers, and he focused his attention on Moscow.

The Soviet leader ignored evidence to the contrary. A German aircraft that carried detailed plans of the southern offensive crashed behind Soviet lines in June. Stalin dismissed the plans as a deliberate attempt by the Germans to mislead them. As they had done before the Germans unleashed Operation Barbarossa, the British provided the Soviets with intelligence that indicated the disposition of the German troops poised for an attack. Stalin, who did not trust the British in 1942 any more than he had in 1941, ignored the intelligence. As a result, the Germans surprised Stalin.

When the Germans opened Operation Blau on 28 June with an offensive in the Kursk area, the Soviets were caught completely off guard. The Soviets did not maintain enough troops in the region to defend it, so the Germans achieved a quick breakthrough and commenced an offensive that seemed destined to repeat the German military performance of the previous summer. On 30 June, the 6th Army, led by General Friedrich von Paulus, began an attack south of the Kursk assault. Instead of insisting that his troops 'stand fast', which would likely have resulted in their annihilation, Stalin, listening to the advice of Zhukov, ordered a retreat. Although Hitler became angry when he learned that the Red Army had not stood fast so that his soldiers could destroy it, he was pleased with the progress that his army made during the first few weeks of the offensive. The Red Army retreated from the area south of Kharkov, and the Crimea fell to the Germans. Initially, Sevastopol, a port on the Black Sea, held out, but it succumbed to overwhelming air and artillery attack on 4 July. (General Erich von Manstein received a promotion to Field Marshal as a result of his troops capturing the city.)

As the German advance into the Caucasus progressed, Stalin assigned Lavrentia Beria, the head of the NKVD (People's Commissariat of Internal Affairs), to the region. Beria's contribution to the defence of the Caucasus was poor, but he did earn a reputation for the severity of his treatment of both Soviet troops and the population of the region. Issuing a 'no retreat' directive, Beria ordered officers to shoot any soldier who withdrew from the line. In addition, Beria's private NKVD army exacted harsh punishment against Kalmyk, Ingush and Chechnyan peasants who failed to support the Soviet cause. The NKVD army, in exercising Beria's wishes, instituted a campaign of mass murder and deportations. Beria's actions would have consequences long after Stalin removed him from the region.

Although he was in good spirits because he thought that the German Army would accomplish what it had failed to do in 1941, Hitler was still impatient. His army did not advance fast enough, and the Red Army refused to stand and fight. Hitler's impatience got the better of him, and he made one of the most important decisions of the war. He relieved

Below: Despite the security risks and the fast-approaching Wehrmacht, Soviet troops parade before Stalin and the Soviet leadership on the anniversary of the Revolution on 7 November 1941.

Above: Hitler had been so confident of a quick victory in the East that the Wehrmacht were not issued with proper winter clothing suitable for the conditions they would face in the Soviet Union.

Below: Extremely low temperatures made fighting during the winter months more difficult. Unlike their opponents, Soviet soldiers were issued with full winter gear which blended into their surroundings.

Field Marshal von Bock from his command of AGS and personally assumed control of Army Group A and Army Group B. Although the German army continued to make gains in July, it again failed in its aim of achieving a decisive victory. Overextension of the front line and logistical problems combined to slow the German advance. Hitler's re-definition of the objectives of Operation Blau meant that the German drive into the Caucasus came to a halt before it could take the oilfields. Hitler changed his priorities and redirected the efforts of Army Group B. After increasing the strength of Army Group B, he ordered it to take Stalingrad, not just to cut it off from the Caucasus. For the first time, Stalingrad became the primary target.

Here again the Führer miscalculated. A number of factors persuaded him to redirect the offensive towards Stalingrad. First, during the opening month of the operation, German troops had captured a large amount of territory, and the Soviet soldiers had appeared to be disorganised. Secondly, in North Africa, German formations under the direction of General Erwin Rommel were pushing British forces back into Egypt. By rapidly taking the Caucasus, Germany could dominate the Middle East. Thirdly, if the Germans succeeded in capturing Stalingrad quickly, they could then proceed to Moscow. Finally, there was the symbolic nature of Stalingrad, scene of Stalin's alleged glory in the Russian Civil War. Up to this point, German forces had failed to surround and crush the Soviet Army. Because he thought that the Red Army might stand and defend Stalingrad, Hitler concluded he could destroy enemy forces there.

On 19 August 1942, the 6th Army and the 4th Panzer Army, led by General Paulus, began the attack on Stalingrad. Within four days, while some German soldiers advanced into the city's suburbs, others reached the Volga north of the city. The citizens living in the southern part of the city began to flee to the east. The Soviet soldiers defending the city began to panic. Then Stalin issued order 'No. 227', in which he ordered the Red Army to stand firm against the invaders. Failure to do so would result in treatment as criminals and deserters. Fierce fighting slowed the Germans' progress into Stalingrad. On 27 August, Stalin appointed Zhukov Deputy Supreme Commander and gave him the task of saving the city. Zhukov very quickly recognised the weaknesses in the German offensive: the army's limited reserves and its long, exposed flanks. He also realised that, by

employing a pincer movement, Soviet forces could isolate the German forces in Stalingrad. By 13 September, Zhukov and Alexander Vasilevsky, the Chief of the General Staff, had devised a plan which they named Operation Uranus. The Soviets would only send enough troops to Stalingrad to prevent the Germans from taking the entire city. In the meantime, they would amass a huge strategic reserve for a well-planned counter-attack that was also logistically well supported.

Two months passed before the Soviets were ready to launch Operation Uranus. During that time, two armies – the 62nd and the 64th – defended the city. When the commander of the 62nd Army began to evacuate his force across the Volga, the commander of the Stalingrad front replaced him with General Vasily Chuikov. Chuikov had assumed command on the same day that Zhukov and Vasilevsky presented

Below: In an effort to keep warm, German troops were forced either to strip the dead of their clothes or improvise with whatever they could find, wearing blanket ponchos and using sheets for camouflage.

Stalin with their preliminary plan for the Soviet counter-offensive. Unlike his colleagues, Chuikov demanded good intelligence, which he used to organise and, when necessary, move his depleted forces to meet any threat posed by the enemy. By the end of October, fierce fighting in the city's factory district had brought both sides to a halt. Paulus gathered his troops for one final attack, which he launched on 9 November. Although the Germans made slight advances in some areas, the assault made little progress overall. When the German advance ground to a halt three days later, Soviet storm troops began to regain lost territory, particularly in the factory district and the centre of town.

On 19 November, the Soviet counter-attack north of Stalingrad began, and caught the Germans completely off guard. A day later, Soviet forces south of

Below: Engaged in fierce street combat, German soldiers cautiously survey their surroundings, looking out for any tell-tale signs of the enemy during the fighting for Stalingrad.

the city hit the German line, which was defended primarily by Romanian and Italian units. Within three days, Soviet mobile units had advanced more than 240km (150 miles), and the two forces met on 22 November. They had Paulus surrounded. Hitler denied his request to surrender and ordered Paulus to 'stand fast'. In addition, Hitler promised that the Luftwaffe would keep Paulus and his men supplied until they were rescued. Unfortunately, the Luftwaffe was incapable of keeping Hitler's promise. On 12 December, the attempt to rescue the beleaguered soldiers began in a heavy rain. Although they made steady progress initially, after engaging in a tank battle with Soviet reinforcements on 23 December, the force could advance no further. Zhukov and the Soviet General Staff had anticipated that the Germans would make such a rescue attempt and had made provisions for it. More than 60 Soviet divisions and 1000 tanks advanced to meet the threat. On 24 December, in danger of being surrounded themselves, the German rescuers retreated and left Paulus and his army to their fate. Because they had greatly underestimated the size of Paulus's force, the Soviets experienced greater difficulty in crushing the Germans' resistance than they had expected. Paulus held out until he had no choice but to surrender on 2 February 1943 – the first German field marshal to do so – which ended the battle for Stalingrad.

With the Soviet victory at Stalingrad, the tide in the East began to turn, but this did not mark the end of the fight. Although the Germans had been defeated, the Soviets did not achieve a decisive victory that would end the war. The Battle of Stalingrad demonstrated the Soviets' improvement in operational skills, and their victory provided the basis for the decisive battle of 1943. The Germans would try to mount an offensive again in the summer of 1943, but this time the Soviets would not be caught by surprise. They would discover what the Germans planned to do and would be ready for them. It would be the Germans who were caught off guard instead. Between the end of January and the beginning of July, with the exception of a battle at Kharkov in March, both the Soviets and the Germans focused their preparations on their next major showdown: the battle of Kursk.

Right: A posed photograph showing Soviet soldiers during the struggle for Stalingrad. Months of hard fighting had reduced the city to rubble in which small groups of soldiers fought in bitter close-quarter combat.

CHAPTER TWO

Planning and Preparation

The German Perspective

Defeat at Stalingrad seriously upset the German plans for victory in the East. Doubts began to arise in the minds of some about the likelihood of final victory, but Hitler planned for Germany's triumph in 1943.

The battle of Stalingrad ended when the last of the 6th German Army capitulated on 2 February 1943, which was three days after the newly promoted Field Marshal Friedrich von Paulus had surrendered. As had happened in 1941, the Germans failed to defeat the Soviets in a single decisive battle. After making major gains at the beginning of the campaign, the attacking Germans became overextended, and their supply lines became tenuous. Winter conditions made the transportation of munitions, food and other materials to the front line extremely difficult. Taking advantage of the Germans' weaknesses, the Soviets handed their enemy another defeat, but it was not a decisive defeat which would end the war in the East. In fact, the Soviet counter-attack at Stalingrad was only one part of a much more ambitious offensive campaign. The Soviet General Staff wanted to press their advantage and push back the entire German front, which stretched from the Baltic Sea to the Black Sea.

Although he had allowed his generals to organise and implement the defence of Stalingrad, Stalin became impatient with the pace of the battle. Consequently, he took back direct control of the offensive from the General

Left: A German StuG III assault gun passes a burning Russian hamlet in the spring of 1943. The Soviet counteroffensive after victory at Stalingrad was beginning to lose momentum when Manstein launched his attack on Kharkov.

Staff. Stalin demanded that the Red Army accomplish more, and at a quicker pace. He wanted the Germans driven out of the Soviet Union. Soviet forces made advances all along the front. They pushed the Germans farther away from Moscow and, in the north, broke the thousand-day German siege of Leningrad. Pleased with the performance of the Red Army, Stalin urged his generals to continue to drive the Germans westwards. With the successes along the front colouring his judgment, Stalin began

to envision victory in a great battle that would collapse the entire German front. As a result, he wanted even bigger gains. However, after the early successes, the Soviets found themselves overextended, poorly supplied and vulnerable. They were not yet at the point at which they could defeat the Germans in one decisive campaign.

Hoping to cut off the German force in the Caucasus, Stalin ordered the Red Army to advance to Rostov. As the Germans' Army Group A had already begun to withdraw, the Soviet commanders in the south received orders to pursue the enemy. The Soviets focused much of their attack to the west and north towards the Kursk and Kharkov areas. In late January and early February, the advancing Soviets attempted to cut off the Germans. Realising the danger, Field Marshal Erich von Manstein, the commander of Army Group South (AGS), ordered a retreat against Hitler's orders, a move that almost cost him his job. By ordering a fighting retreat, however, Manstein accomplished two important things. First, he succeeded in holding the front at Rostov long enough to allow Army Group A to escape. Secondly, he saw the chance to draw the Soviets into a trap and launch a counter-attack.

Despite the heavy losses that they suffered, first at Stalingrad, and then all along the front, the Germans still prepared to attack. Hitler rushed what reserves

Below: Not even the thickness of a forest can stop a T-34 in early 1943. By this stage of the war Soviet factories were producing hundreds of T-34s each month, significantly out-producing their German rivals.

Above: Advancing Waffen-SS troops wearing their winter uniforms accompany a StuG III assault gun during an attack on a Russian village in March 1943 during the Kharkov offensive.

he could to the front. He ordered SS panzer units equipped with a daunting new weapon – the Mark VI 'Tiger' tank – to help Manstein regain the initiative. As the Soviets drove the Germans westwards, a salient developed in the line near Kharkov. Manstein amassed his new reserve forces near Kharkov. The Soviets did not realise that they were walking into a trap. The troops within the salient were flushed with victory; they had made great gains against the enemy. Neither Stalin nor the Soviet General Staff believed that the Germans had the resources to mount an assault. The Soviets had the Germans on the run, or so they thought, and they expected their enemy to continue to retreat towards Germany.

On 20 February 1943, Manstein launched his counter-offensive at Kharkov. His troops hit the overextended Soviet line, which had weak flank support in a very narrow salient. The Soviets were at the very end of their logistical support. By mid-March, the Germans had recaptured Kharkov and began to drive the Soviets back in the direction from which they had come. As the Germans re-stabilised their position and the front line moved eastwards again, part of the Soviet Red Army found itself in another vulnerable position: the Kursk salient. The spring

thaw, or *rasputiza*, came in early April, and both the Germans and the Soviets settled down to regroup, rest, refit their depleted ranks and plan their summer offensives while the roads remained impassable.

As Hitler reviewed Germany's position in April 1943, the picture was not very bright. Wartime-related economic problems had begun to create discontent in Germany. In addition to Stalingrad, German forces had suffered defeat in North Africa at the hands of the British and the Americans, and Germany was losing the fight to maintain its success against the Allied convoys in the Atlantic Ocean. Neither Turkey nor Japan seemed willing or able to join the war against the Soviet Union, and allies such as Italy and Romania began to investigate ways to abandon the apparently sinking ship. The war's momentum appeared to be shifting to the enemy. In Hitler's mind, losing the initiative on the Eastern Front would cause irreparable political damage.

The losses suffered in the 1942–1943 campaign, however, limited the Führer's options. The German

Above: The Soviet rasputiza, *or thaw, turns roads into rivers of mud, like the muddy trenches and roads in Belgium during World War I. Mechanised vehicles would sink into the mud and/or break down.*

High Command (OKH) realised that it could not mount a major strategic offensive on the Eastern Front. That did not mean, however, that it should abandon the idea of a summer offensive. Manstein and other commanders believed that, at the end of the winter campaign, the Germans had a slight advantage over the Soviets, and it was an advantage that should be exploited as soon as the *rasputiza* ended in late April or early May. As the German military staff studied a map of the front, a particular part of the line – the Kursk salient – looked increasingly attractive as a site for a limited offensive. The salient was 250km (155 miles) wide and 160km (100 miles) deep. Not only would the elimination of the salient shorten the front line by 250km (155 miles), but it would also release 18–20 Germans divisions for other operations elsewhere in the East or on some other front. The new Chief of the Army High Command, Colonel General Kurt Zeitzler, suggested an attack on the salient. If the Germans attacked the

bulge at the shoulders, they could wipe out a large number of Soviet soldiers in a large battle of annihilation without becoming overextended. German troops could conceivably destory two Soviet fronts while opening a large hole in the line. The more the military leaders considered the possibilities offered by an offensive at Kursk, the more attractive it became. A victory at Kursk would open the door to the Caucasus and provide both natural resources and prestige, which would demonstrate to the world that Germany was still strong.

The planning for the summer offensive actually began in March. By the middle of the month, the leaders of the OKH issued Operations Order 5, in which they explained the basic premise behind the proposed offensive, which they named Operation Citadel. In devising the plan, the German High Command had to take a number of factors into consideration. First, the Soviets would be making their own plans for a summer offensive: the Germans had to strike before the Soviets were ready to attack. Therefore, Manstein advised launching their assault as soon as the *rasputiza* ended in late April or early May. Secondly, by attacking as soon as the spring thaw had ended, the Germans would have the added advantage of building on the momentum that they had begun to establish when they had pushed the Soviets to the east and recaptured Kharkov in March. Finally, army leaders had to take into account the manpower and equipment shortages that existed as a result of the campaigns of the previous two years. The battle of Stalingrad had caused losses that the Germans had not yet been able to replace. Therefore, the OKH recommended a plan that entailed troops holding most of the line while the armies in AGS delivered limited but powerful attacks. The proposed Operation Citadel offered the perfect option.

Although he accepted the OKH's advice about an offensive against the Kursk bulge, Hitler did not immediately abandon the idea of a more extensive summer campaign. He entertained a series of operations, such as Habicht and Panther, that called for attacks designed to eliminate the Soviet presence in the industrial area of the River Donetz. Hitler eventually rejected these plans, as he decided that they would hinder the pursuit of Operation Citadel. He did, however, recognise the possibility of using Habicht and Panther for deceptive purposes to increase the chances of success at Kursk.

The principal strategic mission of Operation Citadel was the destruction of the Red Army's large force in the Kursk region. Once the Red Army had been destroyed, the German Army could then turn to the north and advance on Moscow from the south. One German army would concentrate its forces around Orel to the north of Kursk and attack

Above: A German motorcyclist demonstrates the perils of attempting to travel on Russian roads in the raputiza. *Twice a year all meaningful attacks ground to a halt as the roads remained largely impassable.*

Below: A propaganda photograph purporting to show Russian partisans attacking a German-held village in 1943. Although partisan groups did exist, they were not yet well-equipped or organised.

southwards, and a second force would amass near Belgorod and move north against the Soviet forces positioned south of Kursk. When the two forces met, they would have effectively cut off Soviet troops in the Kursk salient. To accomplish this, the German armies would deliver powerful, concentric blows from the Orel and Belgorod regions. In doing so, they would eliminate enemy forces along the line of the River Oskol and further north. Following the destruction of the Soviets within the salient, the Germans would bring up fresh reserves, turn to the north-east and surround Moscow from the south and south-east, in conjunction with an attack on the city from the west.

According to the plan, Army Group Centre (AGC) and Army Group South (AGS) were to assemble their panzer forces on the flanks of the bulge by mid-April. As soon as *rasputiza* ended, they would launch a two-pronged assault to close off the bulge. Operations Order 6, issued on 15 April, informed the commanders of the armies implementing Citadel to

Below: A Junkers Ju87 Stuka is loaded with bombs prior to take off on 13 April 1943. The Stuka was a slow cumbersome aircraft, and was extremely vulnerable to the latest Soviet fighters.

be ready to launch the offensive on six days' notice, any time after 28 April. According to the order, the army groups involved had to complete their preparations in time to launch the offensive by the end of the month. The earliest date on which Citadel could begin was 3 May.

Once the German High Command had a plan, they had to make preparations. One of the most important aspects of the preparations was rebuilding the ground forces. The armies on the Eastern Front, however, needed more than manpower. They had suffered losses in tanks, vehicles, weapons, equipment and ammunition: the materials essential for waging war. None of these materials was easy to replace. As much as possible, the armies utilised captured weapons and equipment, but they were insufficient to replace the losses. In addition, using captured vehicles and equipment created the problem of finding replacement parts. Solving the supply problem fell to Albert Speer. With Hitler's ultimate decision to bring total war to Germany, Speer received the job of implementing it in industry. Speer's solution was to redirect industry to war production. In other words, Speer, as a representative of the government, demanded that factories produce

Above: One of the Germans' secret weapons for the Kursk offensive, the PzKpfw V Panther tank. The tank shown is actually a later command variant, identifiable by the antenna behind the tank's commander.

larger quantities of the materials needed to pursue the war.

Government pressure resulted in the rise of production levels. German factories manufactured more than twice as many tanks and assault guns than they had produced a year earlier. The monthly production of rifles and machine pistols increased by almost 50 per cent, while that of machine guns and artillery pieces doubled. Along with increased production, industry felt the pressure to produce better tanks, artillery pieces and weapons of all types. Under Speer's direction, industry rose to the challenge. In 1943, soldiers fighting at Kursk had the MG42, a new light machine-gun that was better than any they had previously used. They also had the benefit of heavier anti-tank guns. Two new tanks – the Tiger and the Panther – rolled off the assembly lines and onto the battlefields in 1943. The Germans used the heavier Tiger tanks to form special battalions that were designed to lead attacks. Tigers, which had heavy armour and 88mm (3.46in) guns, performed well against the Soviet tanks. The Panther tank began to replace the older Mark IV models as the foundation of the panzer divisions. Its 75mm (2.95in) gun gave the Panther the ability to destroy other tanks. In

addition to the Tiger and the Panther, the Germans utilised two other tanks at Kursk: the Panzer III and the Panzer IV. While the Panzer III was equipped with a 50mm (1.97in) anti-tank gun, the Panzer IV had a high-velocity 75mm (2.95in) gun. Both types of tanks had proven themselves on the battlefield. The Germans also produced various assault guns, such as 105mm (4.13in) Wespe (Wasp) and 150mm (5.90in) Hummel (Bumblebee) howitzers, which provided support for the infantry during the offensive. Another new weapon was the 88mm (3.45in) armed Ferdinand (or Elefant) tank destroyer, which was to prove ineffective. However, although German factories produced more than they had in previous years, they still could not manufacture enough to replace obsolete weapons and battlefield casualties, and the better quality weapons had to be used in conjunction with older ones. Despite the improvements in weaponry and firepower, the Germans could not match what the Soviets brought to the battle, particularly in terms of tanks and artillery.

Above: With a new offensive due to begin in the summer of 1943, German factories, under the direction of Albert Speer, implement the changes necessary to increase their tank production.

While replacing lost equipment was important, replenishing manpower was crucial if the Germans ever hoped to launch Citadel. Shortages of weapons, munitions, tanks, vehicles, horses and other equipment delayed the rebuilding process, but without manpower, mounting the summer offensive would be impossible. Between June 1941 and 1 July 1943, the Germans' replacement of troops had not matched their losses. While casualties suffered by the Wehrmacht on all fronts numbered almost four million, the combination of new recruits and wounded who returned to the different fronts only replaced three-quarters of the losses in manpower. During three major operations, the Soviets had destroyed 32 German divisions; the Germans lost 20 of them at Stalingrad. By 1 July 1943, although Germany had 243 divisions in the field, these formations were each short an average of 2500 men. The heavy losses, combined with a fear of the Soviet Union's growing power, brought about a fundamental change in German strategy that began to emerge early in 1943.

On 13 January 1943, Hitler announced for the first time that Germany would devote itself to total war. He instituted a number of policies designed to bring about an economy that could support it. Hitler increased the number of hours in the average working week to 80 and reduced the number of military service exemptions granted to students. The government demanded more women demonstrate their loyalty to the Fatherland by joining the work force, enabling an increased number of men to represent their country on the front lines. The Wehrmacht estimated that at least 800,000 men were needed to replace the losses of the 1942–1943 winter offensive alone; therefore, the government took steps to increase the number of conscripts. The military instituted the induction of members of the Class of 1925 (who were 18 years old). Some men, because of the nature of their employment in the domestic economy, industry or coal-mining sectors, had previously received deferments from the military. Many of these lost their exemption because of the need for more men for the front line. The number of new inductees fell short of the 800,000 needed; therefore, the military decided to enlist 200,000 older men. Although half of them initially came from the

21–37 and 38–42 age groups, within a short time the military leaders realised that they had not reached their goal. Consequently, the Wehrmacht turned to even older men – first to those in their forties, and then, later, to those 50 and older – to make up the difference. Hitler also approved the conscription of individuals of German ancestry who lived in occupied territories, as well as that of foreigners and prisoners of war. The Wehrmacht used these men in their Replacement Army and in railroad construction crews in order to free more 'true' Germans for the front lines. While some of the foreigners and prisoners of war were conscripted, others, after experiencing the camps, volunteered to serve. When women, teenage boys and girls (some as young as 15), and foreigners began to man anti-aircraft weapons around Germany, more men found themselves on active duty at the front.

During the period January to March 1943, German casualties on the Eastern Front numbered 689,260, while only 370,700 soldiers joined the forces on the front line. The leaders of the OKH, who began to address the problem as early as January 1943, realised that replacements from Germany alone could not solve the problem, particularly if they hoped to launch another offensive in the summer. They straightened out the front by eliminating several small salients. The troops that held these areas received orders to transfer to the south. Furthermore, the OKH revised its treatment of training companies. After receiving only eight weeks of preparation, the training companies joined training battalions for an additional eight weeks of instruction. These battalions then joined reserve divisions and helped to maintain order in occupied territories while they continued their preparations for front-line duty. German divisions situated in the West received orders transferring them to the East. Many of the divisions that had been sent to France for rest and rehabilitation returned to the Eastern Front. Between December 1942 and June 1943, Hitler removed all but one combat-ready division from France; he sent the rest to the Soviet Union. In addition, the divisions that remained in France underwent changes. The Wehrmacht sent older conscripts to France to replace the younger men, who were reassigned to divisions on the Eastern Front.

The mainstay of the German defensive force was the infantry, while the panzer forces held the offensive power in the German Army. However, both the

Below: As the time for the summer offensive approached, German trains carried the new Tiger (seen below) and Panther tanks and Ferdinand tank destroyer to the front line.

infantry and the panzer forces needed men and supplies. The infantry frequently replaced the panzer and motorised divisions on the front line while these formations were refitted with men, weapons and equipment. By May 1943, the Wehrmacht's efforts to resolve its manpower problems resulted in the availability of 9.5 million men for all fronts. Consequently, the Wehrmacht would reorganise and rehabilitate its depleted forces. Despite the Wehrmacht's efforts, however, many of the divisions participating in the summer offensive at Kursk remained under-strength. Many contained only six battalions, instead of the intended nine.

Several factors prevented the divisions from regaining their full strength. The high rate of casualties suffered by German armies in the spring of 1943 greatly exceeded the amount of reserves available to replace them. Instead of agreeing to combine divisions to increase their strength, Hitler dictated the creation of new divisions. The number of divisions available for battle remained more important to the

Below: A Tiger from the Das Reich *Waffen-SS division halts in a Russian town before the offensive. The Germans planned to use the heavily armoured Tigers to lead attacks against the Soviet defences.*

Führer than their quality or combat strength. Consequently, the Wehrmacht had to find other ways, such as reorganisation, to enhance the capabilities of the divisions on the Eastern Front.

As the reorganisation progressed and the OKH prepared for Operation Citadel, the Germans fortified airfields and elevated positions on the Eastern Front, including those at Orel, Belgorod, Kharkov, Briansk, and Poltava. According to the OKH plan, Army Group Centre (AGC) would be responsible for the attack against the northern part of the Kursk bulge. Under Field Marshal Günther von Kluge's direction, the AGC would concentrate 2nd Panzer Army, commanded by Colonel General Rudolf Schmidt, and 9th Army, by Colonel General Walter Model, near Orel, north of the bulge. These forces would be opposite the Soviets' Western, Briansk and Central fronts. The 2nd Panzer Army, which included the LV, LIII and XXXV Army Corps, would establish a defensive position along the Kirov-Zmievka Front. The three corps of the 2nd Panzer Army each contained at least four infantry divisions, and the LIII Army Corps one panzergrenadier division.

The 9th Army consisted of five corps: the XXIII and XX Army Corps and the XXXXI, XXXXVI and

XXXXVII Panzer Corps. Only one of the two infantry divisions in the XXIII Army Corps was at full strength with nine battalions. Three of the four divisions in the XXXXI and XXXXVI Panzer Corps were infantry divisions. The two corps had only one panzer division each. Unlike the other panzer corps, the XXXXVII Panzer Corps consisted of three panzer divisions. The 9th Army had 1450 tanks and assault guns to be utilised for the offensive. In addition, the Supreme High Command held 160 Ferdinand assault guns and 150 Tiger tanks in reserve. According to the plan for Citadel, the XXXXI and XXXXVI Panzer Corps would lead the attack, penetrate the Soviet defences and advance 10–12km (6–7.5 miles) on the first day of the offensive. By the fifth day, the XXXXVII Panzer Corps, which was the strongest formation within the 9th Army, would move through the gap in the Soviet line created by the other panzer corps and continue to the area east of Kursk. The two army corps – XX and XXIII – would protect the flanks of the advancing panzer corps. The 9th Army would proceed southwards and ultimately link with the 4th Panzer Army, which would travel northwards from the region around Belgorod.

Right: Vehicles of Panzer Regiment 35 stand ready for the attack, camouflaged in a forest clearing. The tank on the move is a PzKpfw IV, the mainstay of the German armoured forces in 1943.

Above: A German soldier checks the sights on his MG 42 machine gun. By July 1943, thanks to new production targets, German factories were producing twice as many machine guns as they had in 1942.

Under the Citadel plan, Army Group South (AGS) would direct the attack against the southern part of the Kursk bulge. Commanded by Field Marshal Erich von Manstein, the AGS would situate the 4th Panzer Army, led by Colonel General Hermann Hoth, in the Belgorod region. The 4th Panzer Army, the strongest German force in the Kursk area, was also called Army Detachment Hoth. Hoth's formation contained three corps: the LII Army Corps, the XXXXVIII Panzer Corps and the II SS Panzer Corps. The LII

Army Corps, which was in the left sector of the line and would attack the Soviet 40th Army, contained two full-strength infantry divisions – the 57th and the 332nd – and one division with six battalions – the 255th. The 332nd Infantry Division had not seen much combat and, consequently, was the strongest division in the corps. The XXXXVIII Panzer Corps would hold the centre of the line in the part to the left of the assault area. The corps included three panzer and one infantry division. In the XXXXVIII Panzer Corps sector, the *Grossdeutschland* Panzergrenadier Division would be on the left, the 11th Panzer Division would be in the centre, and the nine battalions of the 167th Infantry Division would be on the right. The corps commander would keep the 3rd Panzer Division in reserve in the area south of Kharkov. The strongest of the 4th Panzer Army's three corps was the II SS Panzer Corps. The II SS Panzer Corps had a Tiger battalion with 45 Tiger tanks. The corps contained three strong SS panzer divisions: the *Leibstandarte Adolf Hitler*, *Das Reich* and *Totenkopf*. Each of these divisions had at least 100 of the latest tanks and 13 attached Tigers.

According to the OKH plan, formations of the II SS and XXXXVIII Panzer Corps would launch the main attack from an area south-east of Tomarovka. A shock group would break out and head for Oboian and Kursk. By the fifth or sixth day, advance elements of the 4th Panzer Army would link with elements of the 9th Army at Kursk. The two armies would capture Kursk by the tenth day of the offensive, and they would gradually destroy the Soviet forces caught within the bulge. The Germans expected to capture a large number of Soviet soldiers, which they would send back to Germany to work in war industries. Once control of Kursk was re-established, the Wehrmacht could transfer divisions back to the West to meet the threat posed by the Americans and the British in North Africa.

The 4th Panzer Army's main problem throughout the offensive would be shortages of infantry troops. The protection of the 4th Panzer Army's eastern flank initially fell to Army Detachment Kempf, which was commanded by General of Panzer Troops Werner Kempf. Army Detachment Kempf contained three corps: III Panzer Corps on the left, Corps Raus south of III Panzer Corps, and XXXXII Army Corps opposite the Soviet 57th Army. The III Panzer Corps contained three panzer divisions and one infantry division. A strong formation in good condition, the III Panzer Corps would play a significant role in the battle. Corps Raus, which included two full-strength infantry divisions, was in excellent condition. It would protect the flank of the attack against the 7th Soviet Guards Army. General Kempf held the XXXXII Army Corps, which included three full-strength infantry divisions, in reserve. Although the original intention had been to use Army Detachment Kempf as a flank guard, this unit would play a key role in Operation Citadel. Unlike the 9th Army and the 4th Panzer Army, Army Detachment Kempf would attack the shoulder of the Soviet defences, not their strong points.

Although the primary assaults against the bulge would come from the north by 9th Army and the south by 4th Panzer Army, Operation Citadel also made provisions for pressure to be applied to the face of the bulge from the west by 2nd Army. Commanded by Colonel General Walter Weiss, the 2nd Army, because of its most recent combat experiences, was much weaker than 9th Army. During the fighting in February and March 1943, the Soviets had decisively beaten the 2nd Army, which had almost been encircled. After the mauling it had received, the 2nd Army, which only had 96,000 men, was incapable of playing a major role at Kursk. Consequently, the 2nd Army, with its seven-plus divisions, received the job of providing a thin screen across the face of the bulge. Weiss divided these divisions, along with three anti-tank detachments, into two army corps: the XIII and VII Army Corps. The two corps, which provided a thin connection between Army Group Centre (AGC) and Army Group South (AGS), played a purely defensive role in the offensive. Two divisions of XIII Corps, along with one regiment from another division, would hold the northern part of 2nd Army's sector. While the 82nd Division held the left, the six battalions of the 340th Infantry Division were situated in the centre of the corps' area. VII Corps was responsible for the southern part of the 2nd Army's sector. Four of the 2nd Army's infantry divisions contained nine weak battalions each. The 88th Infantry Division was located next to XIII Corps. South of the 88th Infantry Division were, from left to right, the 26th, the 75th and the 68th Infantry Divisions. The seven weak infantry divisions had the responsibility of covering a 170km (105 mile) front that faced two Soviet armies, the 6th and the 38th.

As the preparations neared completion, opponents of Operation Citadel, such as Manstein and General Heinz Guderian, expressed their doubts.

Above: Two Waffen-SS soldiers lurking in a field of sunflowers in June 1943. Although the Germans attempted to camouflage their assembly positions, the Soviets had already guessed their offensive plans.

Below: The situation as it stood on the Eastern Front in the spring of 1943, showing the Soviet offensives after Stalingrad, and the German counter-offensives at Kharkov, forming the bulge in the line at Kursk.

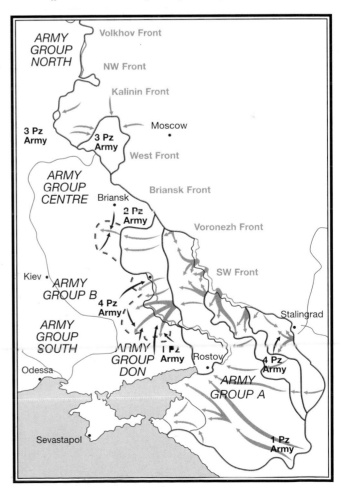

Even Hitler vacillated between support for and opposition to the plan. In response to a suggestion made by Colonel General Kurt Zeitzler, Hitler attended a meeting in Munich on 3 May 1943, the earliest date on which the summer offensive could begin. The topic of discussion was Operation Citadel, which the OKH had delayed on 30 April because the spring rains had not yet ended. Zeitzler wanted Hitler's support because opposition to the plan had arisen. The opponents identified several important problems.

First, for the plan to work, the offensive had to begin as soon as the spring thaw ended and before the Soviets began their summer offensive. The target date had been late April or early May. It was 3 May, but preparations for the offensive remained incomplete. Although he had originally supported the plan, Manstein withdrew his support. He believed that the operation's window of opportunity had passed because it would not begin on time. The field marshal hesitated to vocalise his objections too strongly,

Below: Early July 1943: German armoured commanders, conferring at the front, discuss the implementation of Hitler's orders. Most realised the offensive was a last chance to regain the initiative in the East.

however, as he found it extremely difficult to oppose someone as powerful as the Führer.

Secondly, according to Zeitzler, it did not matter if the offensive began late. After all, newly formed units of Panther and Tiger tanks would spearhead the assault. Colonel General Heinz Guderian had received the task of rebuilding the panzer units that would be used in Citadel. Both Guderian and Speer, who also attended the meeting, pointed out the realities of the situation. The production of these weapons involved numerous technical problems, which meant that the numbers available in time for the offensive would be strictly limited. After receiving Hitler's permission to voice his opinion, Guderian suggested that it would be better to use the new tanks on the Western Front against an invasion than to waste them in a frontal assault at Kursk. Neither Zeitzler nor Field Marshal Günther von Kluge, the commander of Army Group Centre (AGC), listened to Guderian and Speer.

Finally, the commander of the 9th Army, which would make the primary assault, opposed the offensive. General Walter Model produced aerial photographs of the Soviet defences at Kursk. As he pointed out, and the photographs demonstrated, the Soviets expected the Germans to attack at Kursk, and they had constructed an elaborate defensive network to meet this attack. Success would be extremely difficult. The Soviets had not been idle while the Germans had prepared for their new offensive.

The most ardent supporter of the offensive, as it was designed by Zeitzler, was Field Marshal Günther von Kluge. During the meeting he did not even entertain the idea that the Germans could fail in 1943 as they had in 1941 and 1942. According to Kluge, no defences that the Soviets built could withstand an assault by Tiger and Panther tanks. The new tanks could overcome any obstacle. Like the other generals, Kluge realised that technology fascinated Hitler. Consequently, he played down the production problems and emphasised the powerful capabilities of the new tanks in an attempt to gain further favour. The more Kluge voiced his support for Citadel, the more adamantly Guderian opposed it. While most of the general's opposition was justified, his dislike of Kluge intensified it. The disagreement between the two men reached the point where Kluge challenged Guderian to a duel and asked Hitler to be his second. Calmer heads prevailed, and the duel did not take place. The incident did, however, demonstrate

both the dislike the two men felt for each other, and the emotions generated by Operation Citadel.

During the conference, Hitler, as always, took centre stage. He summarised both the plan and Model's objections to it. Although he appeared sympathetic to Model's arguments and did not readily give his support, the Führer also hesitated to oppose Citadel. His indecision with regard to a military operation was, at this stage of the war, uncharacteristic. For two days, Hitler and his generals considered the plan and discussed three options. The Germans had the choice of launching the offensive immediately, or they could delay it, or they could cancel it altogether. The issue remained unresolved at the end of the conference. Moreover, because the OKH did not cancel Citadel, the plan remained in effect, but it lacked a starting date.

The Germans would ultimately launch their summer offensive in July 1943, long after their original target date of 3 May. The OKH delayed Citadel several times between 3 May and 5 July. Various factors caused the delays, but not all of them were related to the Eastern Front. Continual rain brought the first decision to delay on 30 April. The Munich conference ended without a new target date being set. Hitler was concerned enough about tank production, fearing that not enough Panthers and Tigers would be available for the attack, to postpone the operation

Above: A Tiger tank on the edge of an airstrip just before the offensive began. After several false alarms, Hitler finally issued orders on 1 July for the commencement of Operation Citadel.

until 12 June. Guderian met with Hitler and Field Marshal Wilhelm Keitel, the Chief of the Armed Forces Staff, on 10 May. Guderian wanted to preserve materiel and manpower resources for the second front in Western Europe, so he pressed Hitler to cancel Citadel. Keitel argued that political factors dictated the implementation of the offensive. During the discussion, Hitler again expressed concerns, but he did not cancel the plan. On 13 May, after Tunisia fell to Allied forces, the Führer ordered another postponement. Because of the Allies' threat to Italy, he ordered a delay until the end of June.

Although he did consider cancelling the offensive, finally, on 1 July, Hitler issued a special order authorising the start of Operation Citadel. The Germans had delayed their summer offensive for two months, during which time the Soviets continued to construct defences and to prepare for the German attack. Evidence presented by Model on 3 May indicated the extent of the enemy's defensive position around Kursk. The Germans gave the Soviets a further two months to improve their defences, and when Operation Citadel finally began on 5 July, they met a well-prepared enemy.

The Soviet Response

Iron Defences

After their defeat at Kharkov, the Red Army had not been idle. Knowing that a German attack must come, and aided by intelligence, the Soviets thoroughly prepared the defences of the Kursk salient to meet the German threat.

In 1941, when the Germans invaded the Soviet Union, they surprised their enemy, who did not trust British predictions about an impending attack. Operation Barbarossa achieved surprise on all levels: tactical, operational and strategic. The Germans caught the Soviets off guard again in 1942 when they launched Operation Blau, which led to the Battle of Stalingrad. With Operation Blau, the Germans accomplished operational and tactical surprise. While the leaders of the Stavka (Soviet Supreme Command) did expect the Germans to attack, they failed to correctly predict the location of the offensive. Both Stalin and Stavka believed that the Germans would attempt to capture Moscow again; the Germans focused on the Caucasus instead. In each instance, the Soviet forces eventually rallied, halted the German advance, and initiated their own offensives. In both cases, however, the Soviets were overambitious in their counter-attacks and, after initial successes, failed to eliminate the German threat. Stalin and the Soviet military leadership wanted the situation to be different in 1943. In light of recent experience, the Soviets anticipated another German offensive in the spring or summer. The key was to

Left: Soviet forces on the offensive in late 1942. By 1943, despite the setback suffered at Kharkov, the Red Army was far more confident and professional a force than the one beaten so easily by the Wehrmacht in 1941.

ascertain where that offensive would be and hence be prepared. Neither Stalin nor Stavka was willing to allow the Germans to accomplish the advances that they had achieved during the previous two years.

By the time the Germans launched their summer offensive in 1943, the situation in the Soviet Union was vastly different from what it had been in 1941 and 1942. Unlike the earlier campaigns, in which the

German objectives were unrealistic, the Germans set goals in Operation Citadel which were achievable under normal circumstances. Without surprise and air superiority, and with the extensive Soviet

Below: A Soviet tankette with its commander in October 1942. The Soviet Union continued to build such obsolescent vehicles in large numbers despite the proven success of the T-34 tank.

defences throughout the Kursk salient, however, German success became less likely. The German Luftwaffe could no longer claim to have air superiority, which had been the case in 1941. By 1942, the Luftwaffe's air superiority had declined, as the Soviet Air Force began to recover from the losses that it had suffered a year earlier. When Operation Citadel began, both the Germans and the Soviets would fight for air superiority. In addition, by the summer of 1943, Hitler was exerting an increasing amount of direct control over the direction of German campaigns. He deliberately ignored the arguments made by many experienced German commanders – particularly Colonel General Heinz Guderian, General Walter Model, and Field Marshal Erich von Manstein – against launching Citadel. As the Führer increasingly limited the flexible command capabilities of the German military leadership, Josef Stalin moved in the opposite direction, and allowed his commanders more flexibility and influence in the development of the Soviet war strategy.

Before the leaders of Stavka could devise a strategic plan for 1943, they had to assess the Soviet military's performance during the preceding two years. Following each German summer offensive, the Soviets had launched winter counter-offensives. In those of 1941–1942 and 1942–1943, Soviet military leaders tried to do too much too quickly. To a certain extent, their actions were in response to Stalin's demands, but they were also the result of overconfidence in their troops, who had stopped the German advance and forced a retreat. Consequently, the Soviet line became overextended, and the advance of the Soviet armies was first slowed and then stopped because of logistical problems. As they intended to avoid a repeat of past performances, most senior Soviet officers recognised the need to set more modest, realistic goals for the future. A single, climactic offensive was not possible.

In order to develop their own offensive plans, Soviet military leaders also had to determine the Germans' plans. They believed that any attack by the Germans in 1943 would be much more limited in scope than had been the case during the past two years. Soviet leaders concurred that the Germans' losses in manpower and equipment would prevent them from launching an attack on a wide front. As they studied the map, the Soviets came to the same conclusions as their opponents. The Kursk salient was the obvious choice for the location of a limited

Above: Stalin called upon Marshal of the Soviet Union Georgi Konstantinovich Zhukov, the saviour of Moscow and Stalingrad, to apply his skills to the impending battle for the Kursk salient.

offensive, which would shorten the front by 250km (155 miles) and release 18–20 German divisions for action elsewhere. The build-up of German forces both north and south of the salient indicated how correct the Soviet conclusions really were. Once they had determined the logical place for a German offensive, the Soviet commanders had to decide upon the best course of action: strike first, or wait to counterattack when the enemy was overstretched.

While the Stavka was considering strategic plans for 1943, Stalin had his own ideas for the future. He envisioned a summer offensive that included attacks by the Central and Voronezh fronts towards the Dniepr River, which would clear Belorussia, retake Kharkov and liberate Donbas. The placement of German forces, however, made such a plan risky. Stalin and the Stavka generals debated the best course of action. Army General Nikolai Vatutin, the commander of the Voronezh Front, argued for a preemptive strike by Soviet forces before the Germans completed their plans. According to Vatutin, it was

Above: The Red Army on the offensive in the winter of 1942. Better equipped physically and psychologically for the extreme cold than their German counterparts, Soviet troops crawl forward in the snow.

important for the Soviets to regain the momentum that they had lost to the Germans at the end of the 1942–1943 winter campaign. They could not allow the enemy to capitalise on the mistakes that the Soviets had made.

Other general staff officers, such as Marshal of the Soviet Union, Georgi Zhukov and Marshal of the Soviet Union, Alexander Vasilevsky, urged a more cautious approach. Both Zhukov and Vasilevsky took the lead in recommending that the Soviet Army wage a defensive battle to reduce the Germans' striking power. Once the enemy had been sufficiently weakened, the Soviets could then shift to the offensive. While Hitler considered whether or not to proceed with Operation Citadel, Stalin weighed his options. Before he reached a decision, Vasilevsky, as Chief of the General Staff, issued a directive to all front and army commanders ordering them to organise better defensive positions during the *rasputiza* (spring thaw) and to focus particularly on anti-tank positions. Vasilevsky's directive included the creation of reserves and the improvement of force combat training. In addition, the Chief of the General Staff ordered an intensification of intelligence collection. Thus began a massive effort to gather intelligence that did not stop until Citadel began and which focused on the identification of the concentration of enemy forces, as well as the Germans' movement of their operational and strategic reserves, both

between different army groups and from the rear to the front.

On 12 April 1943, in a meeting with Stalin at the Kremlin, Zhukov, Vasilevsky and Colonel General Aleksei Antonov, who was the 1st Deputy Chief of the Red Army General Staff, presented their case. The three commanders emphasised the importance of a temporary defensive to deplete the Germans' attack capabilities. After the enemy had been sufficiently weakened, the Soviet armies could launch their offensive. In addition to reporting his assessment of German troop dispositions and capabilities, Zhukov also presented his recommendation for a strategic plan to Stalin. According to the commander, the Soviets should strengthen their anti-tank defences on the Central and Voronezh fronts. He also advised the immediate assembly of 30 anti-tank artillery regiments, as well as the concentration of as much air strength as possible, in the Supreme Headquarters' reserve. Zhukov further suggested that the Soviets use massed air attacks with tank and rifle units to strike at the enemy's shock forces, an action which would disrupt the Germans' offensive plans. The marshal also presented his and Vasilevsky's proposal for the disposition of operational and strategic reserves. Zhukov concluded by reiterating the majority position on the best strategy: wear the enemy down with the defences, destroy the enemy's tanks, move up fresh Soviet reserves and then launch an offensive.

Although he preferred to strike first by launching an attack immediately after the *rasputiza*, Stalin ultimately accepted the recommendation of Zhukov,

Vasilevsky and Antonov, which represented the opinion of the majority of the members of Stavka. Once Stalin agreed to the defensive first strategy, the leaders of Stavka could finalise their strategic plans. The plan for the 1943 summer–autumn campaign assigned the defence of the Kursk salient to the Voronezh and Central fronts, which were commanded by Vatutin and Army General Konstantin Rokossovsky, respectively. The Briansk Front, led by Colonel General Markian Popov, and Western Front, under Colonel General Vasily Sokolovsky, would protect the northern flank, while Colonel General Rodion Malinovsky's South-western Front would do the same on the southern flank. Stalin agreed to the creation of a large strategic reserve, the Steppe Front, and approved the assignment of the command to Colonel General Ivan Konev. Konev's forces would play a crucial role at Kursk.

The Stavka ordered all fronts to erect strong defences, as the Soviet military leaders remained uncertain about the exact nature of the German offensive. From the beginning, these defensive preparations were an important part of the plan for a subsequent Soviet offensive. Improvements to the Soviet defences began after mid-April, demonstrating the commitment to Stavka's strategic plan to

implement a defensive strategy before going on the offensive. However, Soviet preparations involved much more than the strengthening of the defences in and behind the Kursk salient.

The offensives of 1941, 1942 and early 1943 had taken their toll on the Soviets, as they had on the Germans. Both combatants suffered heavy losses in men and materiel. Replacing the losses in equipment – tanks, other motorised vehicles, weapons and ammunition – provided a real challenge to the Soviets. The Soviet approach to the design and production of armoured vehicles differed from that of the Germans. While the Germans continually developed new tanks, the Soviets focused on the production of two tanks: the T-34 medium tank and the KV-1 heavy tank. Because of their emphasis on increased production levels, the Soviets made few technical improvements to these tanks. They made only one major attempt to design a new, universal tank, between 1942 and 1943, but the introduction of the Tiger tank to the battlefield by the Germans forced the project's abandonment. Despite heavy losses

Below: The Soviets were masters of salvaging useful equipment left on the battlefield. Here a Red Army sergeant removes the machine gun from a knocked-out German PzKpfw II tank in late 1942.

Above: Soviet gunners practise loading their M1942 ZIS-3 76mm (3in) anti-tank gun. Soviet artillery had also improved dramatically since the beginning of the war in the Soviet Union.

between June 1941 and December 1942, in early 1943, the Soviets' vehicle inventory still included 20,600 tanks. This was because, while the Germans tried to improve their tanks, the Soviets focused more on quantity. Consequently, the Soviets brought many more tanks to the battle at Kursk than the Germans did; however, the quality of the German tanks, in most cases, was superior to that of the Soviet enemy. In 1943, the Soviets supplemented their supply of light reconnaissance tanks with those supplied by the British, Canadians and Americans through the Lend-Lease programme. By July 1943, the

Below: Overcoat-clad Soviet troops move slowly through the snow, poised to provide infantry support for an advancing T-34 during the fighting on the Lower Don front in January 1943.

Soviets received approximately 6000 tanks from their allies. The British sent surplus Churchills, Grants and Stuarts, some of which saw action at Kursk. More important than the tanks provided by the Soviet Union's allies were the Lend-Lease trucks and jeeps, which made a major contribution during the course of the battle. Both were extremely useful, especially providing much-needed logistical support at Kursk.

In addition to tanks, trucks and jeeps, the Soviets required anti-tank weapons at Kursk to meet the threat posed by the Germans. By the summer of 1943, Soviet troops had access to anti-tank weapons that were much improved over those used in early campaigns. By March 1943, Soviet industry began production of the SU-152, designed to destroy heavy German tanks such as the Tiger. Although the new weapons were effective against some of the German tanks, they were not adequate for frontal assaults against the new German Panther and Tiger tanks. The greatest weakness of the Soviet Army, however, was in infantry anti-tank weapons. Many of these weapons were obsolete, which forced the Soviet infantry to adopt almost suicidal tactics against tanks.

In the months before Operation Citadel opened, both the Germans and the Soviets used the time to prepare. Only part of the preparations concerned building up supplies of tanks, other motorised vehicles, rifles, anti-tank weapons, ammunition and other necessities of battle. Although amassing the tools of war and developing an offensive or a defensive strategy were crucial, these things would not matter if the commanders did not have the soldiers to carry out their plans. Both the German and the Soviet forces

Above: Another example of Soviet resourcefulness: a captured PzKpfw III covered in patriotic slogans leads captured StuG III assault guns towards the front to be used against their former owners.

suffered heavy casualties in two years of brutal fighting on the Eastern Front. While the Germans were to find it difficult to replace their losses, however, the Soviets had a vast population upon which to draw replacement troops. Between June 1941 and November 1942, the strength of the Soviet Army increased from 2.9 to 6.1 million men. The high casualties did not have the same devastating effect on the Soviets' ability to continue the war as it did on the Germans. Troop shortages limited the scope of the Germans' 1943 summer offensive, but the Soviets did not suffer from the same constraints. What limited the Soviets in the first few years of the war was not the lack of manpower, but the lack of an effective strategy to meet the German threat.

Although the Germans continued to view the Soviets as inept on the battlefield, by the time the two forces met at Kursk, the Soviet Army had begun to implement changes based upon its experiences against the Germans. Intending to learn from their mistakes, special staff officers compiled extensive after-action reports, and all levels of the Soviet command structure had access to the conclusions reached based upon these reports. By 1943, the army in the field was a flexible unit that could be altered for almost every situation with the attachment of tanks, self-propelled artillery, artillery, anti-tank guns, anti-aircraft guns or other supporting units.

Soviet commanders shifted the supporting units to the areas where they were most needed.

Like the field armies, the tank units underwent essential changes. One of the major weaknesses of the Soviet military was the inability of the tank and mechanised corps to execute deep raids. Consequently, in January 1943, Stalin approved the formation of five tank armies. The T-34/76 tank provided the backbone of these armies. The goal was to create tank armies that had the ability to engage in independent, deep operations. By April, the Stavka began to form artillery breakthrough corps and anti-tank regiments to be used in breakthrough operations. The creation of tank armies or artillery breakthrough corps alone did not guarantee success: the tank armies needed independent officers who could develop the tactics appropriate for battle against the German panzer armies. One such commander was Lieutenant General Pavel Rotmistrov of the 5th Guards Tank Army. Rotmistrov developed tank units that utilised deception, surprise attack and unconventional methods when possible.

In addition to constructing defences and amassing ground and tank forces, the Soviets also built up

Above: Trying to avoid breathing in the dust thrown up by its tracks, infantrymen ride on a T-34 which is making its way out to the front lines. Handholds were provided on later Soviet tank models.

their air forces. During Barbarossa and Blau, they suffered the effects of German air superiority. In 1941, the enemy destroyed 2000 Soviet aircraft on the ground at the start of Barbarossa, and German aircraft dominated the skies, although they did so to a lesser extent in 1942. By the summer of 1943, the Luftwaffe's glory had begun to wane. This was evident in 1942 when the Luftwaffe could not fulfill Hitler's promise of keeping the German forces which were surrounded in Stalingrad supplied with food, ammunition and equipment until they were rescued. These forces did not receive the much-needed supplies, and rescue forces failed to reach them. At Kursk, the Luftwaffe suffered from a shortage of both aircraft and fuel. The lack of fuel, in particular, prevented the German air forces from providing the ground troops with close air support at a time when this was essential for success on the ground.

As the Luftwaffe declined in strength and effectiveness, the Soviet Army Air Force (VVS) underwent enormous improvements in 1942, under the direction of Marshal Alexander Novikov. Following the premise that at least one air army should support each front, Novikov eventually created 17 air armies, and he expected all operational plans to be devised by front and air army commanders working together in order to achieve full service cooperation. The Stavka approved the creation of three strategic forces, as well as a service maintenance command, which would be directly subordinated to the central command. In addition, the Soviet Air Force formed a formidable strategic reserve. Novikov ordered three

air armies to support the most threatened areas: the Central and Voronezh fronts. The 16th Air Army, commanded by Colonel General S. Rudenko, provided support for the Central Front. The 2nd Air Army, under Colonel General S. Krasovsky, and the 17th Air Army, led by Colonel General V. Sudets, supported the Voronezh Front. The Stavka's reserve and the 15th Air Army on the Briansk Front provided additional support.

The primary mission of the VVS was to provide tactical support for the ground forces with light and attack bombing, reconnaissance and fighter operations. Novikov and Stavka envisaged two phases of the air offensive. During the first phase, the VVS would pave the way for ground forces with heavy strikes against enemy airfields and supply lines. In the second phase, the VVS would provide close support, while continuing to attack tactical targets in the enemy's rear. The primary weapon of the VVS was the Ilyushin IL-2 Shturmovik, a ground-attack aircraft with a reputation for durability and armoured protection. By the summer of 1943, the Soviets had introduced the Ilyushin IL-2m3, with a more powerful engine, a rear gunner position with a 12.7mm (0.5in) machine gun and two 37mm (1.46in) cannons mounted on the wings and capable of penetrating the armour of most German tanks. The IL-2m3 surpassed the IL-2. By 1943, the Soviets had fighters in the air that were comparable to those used by the Germans. The new Lavochkin LA-5FN went into service at Kursk. The LA-5FN had a speed that was equivalent to, or even surpassed, that of the German FW-190A-4 and the Bf-109G-4. In addition, the Soviets employed the Yak-9 fighter in the campaign. When the Soviets launched their counter-offensive at Kursk, they had a 5:1 superiority in aircraft. The VVS put 2000 aircraft in the air to the Germans' 400. While the Soviet Air Force would not dominate the skies at Kursk, neither would the Luftwaffe; however, both air forces would achieve local successes.

The Stavka based its preparations at Kursk on the concept of elastic defence. The purpose of an elastic defence was to limit the effectiveness of an enemy artillery barrage by scattering defensive positions in the main line of resistance in a series of strong points. If the defences were properly constructed, most of the enemy shells would not fall on entrenched troops. Key to the Soviet success at Kursk was the depth of the defensive system built between March and late June 1943. These defences,

Above. T-34s wait for orders during the fighting for Kharkov in March 1943. The wide tracks of the T-34 gave it a low ground pressure, which meant that it could cross soft ground or snow easily.

especially those within the salient, were the most elaborate ever built by the Soviets during the war.

As the Stavka's representatives, Zhukov and Vasilevsky organised the defences within and behind the Kursk salient. They determined the disposition of the forces in the region and oversaw all aspects of the campaign. Although they initially focused on the defensive nature of the early campaign, Zhukov, Vasilevsky and other members of Stavka also had to determine where to mount their offensive when the time came. The German salient around Orel, which was north of Kursk, provided excellent possibilities. If timed correctly, a Soviet attack on the forces around Orel could thwart the assault towards Kursk by Army Group Centre (AGC) and ultimately collapse the Orel salient. Consequently, the Stavka placed almost as much importance on Sokolovsky's Western Front and Popov's Briansk Front, which opposed AGC, as it did on the forces within the Kursk bulge.

In order to implement the Stavka's plan, Colonel General Sokolovsky positioned two armies from his Western Front, supported by elements of the 1st Air Army, to face the German 2nd Panzer Army. He deployed Lieutenant General Ivan Bagramian's 11th Guards Army in the area north-west of Orel, assigning it the task of spearheading the decisive Western Front thrust towards the important Briansk–Orel rail line. On Bagramian's left flank, the 50th Army, commanded by Lieutenant General I. V. Boldin, would support the 11th Guards Army's main offensive efforts with 54,062 men, 87 tanks and self-propelled guns, and 1071 guns and mortars. Sokolovsky also had two tank corps – I and V Tank Corps – to put into the line when needed, and the 11th Army held in reserve.

Colonel General Markian Popov's Briansk Front would launch the second part of the assault on the Orel salient. Three of Popov's armies – the 3rd, the 61st and the 63rd – would play an important role at Orel. Popov placed the 3rd Army, commanded by Lieutenant General A. V. Gorbatov, opposite the tip of the salient. The 3rd Army would lead the attack against the line and head westwards for Orel. The 63rd Army, commanded by Lieutenant General V. I. Kolpakchi and positioned on the right flank of 3rd Army, would join in the direct assault on Orel during the counter-attack phase. The final participant in the initial assault was Lieutenant General P. A. Belov's 61st Army, which established its defences in the area between the 63rd and 11th Guards Armies. Containing 80,000 men and 110 tanks, the 61st Army anticipated another opportunity to tangle with the enemy. Popov's Briansk Front received support from the 15th Air Army and the Stavka's reserve forces, including the XXV Rifle Corps, I Guards Tank Corps, two full artillery penetration corps and other support units. With its reinforcements, the Briansk Front numbered 433,616 men, 847 tanks and self-propelled guns, 7642 guns and mortars, and approximately 1000 supporting aircraft. Other new units, held in reserve by the Stavka, would provide additional support for both the Western and Briansk fronts. These units included the 11th Army, with 65,000 men and commanded by Lieutenant General I. I. Fediuninsky; Lieutenant General Pavel Rybalko's 3rd Guards Tank Army, with a force of 731 tanks and self-propelled guns; the 652 tanks and self-propelled guns of Lieutenant General Vasily Badanov's 4th Tank Army; the XX and XXV Separate Tank Corps; and the II Guards Cavalry Corps.

The most important Soviet defences were those within the Kursk salient. Army General Konstantin Rokossovsky and the Central Front had the responsibility of protecting the northern half of the bulge, the area slated to be attacked by the German 9th Army, and the general organised his defences accordingly. The Central Front contained five rifle armies – the 48th, the 13th, the 70th, the 65th and

Below: A Soviet observation team check German positions in the spring of 1943 as they wait for the summer offensive to begin. They are sheltering under a knocked-out German PzKpfw IV tank.

60th Armies – as well as the 2nd Tank and 16th Air Armies and the IX and XIX Tank Corps. Rokossovsky also had a large reserve of armoured and rifle formations, with which he could mount counter-attacks. Rokossovsky placed three full rifle armies in the first and second army defensive belts. Lieutenant General I. V. Galanin's 70th Army, Lieutenant General N. P. Pukhov's 13th Army and Lieutenant General P. L. Romenenko's 48th Army had the responsibility of constructing and manning these important defences. Soviet intelligence sources indicated that the brunt of the German attack from the north would fall on the 13th Army, which had seen little action up to this point. Initially, 11 rifle divisions, 1 tank brigade, 5 tank regiments, 2 anti-aircraft divisions and 1 three-division artillery corps formed the 13th Army.

As a result of the projected German assault, the 13th Army also received six more divisions, including three guards rifle divisions in April and May; and three guards airborne divisions in May. In addition, the 13th Army had a strong tank component and a large artillery component. With the reinforcements, Pukhov commanded 114,000 men, 270 tanks and self-propelled guns, and 2934 guns and mortars. Galanin's 70th Army and Romenenko's 48th Army provided flank support for the 13th Army. Situated on the left flank, Galanin's force, which consisted of

Above: Soviet anti-tank gunners jump from their US-supplied M3A1 Scout Car. By 1943 the Soviet Union was receiving large quantities of supplies and equipment from their American and British allies.

eight rifle divisions and three tank regiments, included 96,000 men, 125 tanks and 1678 guns and mortars. Located on the 13th Army's right flank, Romenenko's 48th Army had seven rifle divisions, six tank and self-propelled artillery regiments, and various supporting units with a total strength of 84,000 men, 178 tanks and self-propelled guns, and 1545 guns and mortars.

Rokossovsky deployed his other armies – Lieutenant General I. D. Cherniakhovsky's 60th and Lieutenant General P. I. Batov's 65th – in the wider segments of the western face of the bulge, opposite the enemy's 2nd Army. Between them, the two armies provided 196,000 men for the defence of the salient. Rokossovsky's front had more than 1500 tanks and 91 self-propelled artillery (SUs) against the 9th Army's six panzer divisions and other armoured units that contained 600 operational tanks and 280 assault guns. Held in reserve, the 2nd Tank Army, under Lieutenant General Aleksei Rodin, contained the III and XVI Tank Corps and the 11th Guards Tank Brigade and had a strength of 37,000 men and 477 tanks and self-propelled guns.

The 4th Panzer Army had the job of leading the attack against the southern part of the Kursk salient in the Voronezh Front area. Commanded by Army General Nikolai Vatutin, the Voronezh Front contained three rifle armies: the 38th, the 40th and the 69th Armies. In addition to the three rifle armies, the Voronezh Front included the 6th Guards Army and 7th Guards Army, the 1st Tank Army, the 2nd Air

Army and three corps: the XXXV Guards Rifle, the II Guards Tank and the V Guards Tank Corps. Vatutin's front had a total of 625,591 men, 1704 tanks and self-propelled guns, and 8718 guns and mortars. The 1st Tank Army, with 646 tanks and self-propelled guns, provided the armoured centre of Vatutin's force. The Voronezh commander assigned the job of defending the wide fronts to the west and south-west against the enemy's 2nd Army to Lieutenant General N. E. Chibisov's 38th Army and Lieutenant General K. S. Moskalendo's 40th Army. While the 38th Army contained six rifle divisions and two tank brigades, the 40th Army had seven rifle divisions, two tank brigades and a heavy tank regiment. The two forces accounted for 137,000 men, 219 tanks and more than 2500 guns and mortars.

The 6th Guards Army and 7th Guards Army, both of which were battle-worn, received the task of defending the front against the main attack by the 4th Panzer Army and Army Detachment Kempf. Both armies had 7 divisions grouped into 2 rifle corps and a variety of tank and anti-tank artillery units, as well as 20 artillery regiments. Both Lieutenant General I. M. Chistiakov's 6th Guards Army and Lieutenant General M. S. Shumilov's 7th Guards Army each had a combined strength of 16,000 men and 401 tanks and self-propelled guns. Although the 13th Army in the northern part of the salient had a narrow area of the front to defend, the 6th Guards Army and 7th Guards Army had to defend much larger portions of the line with fewer resources. The 6th Guards Army

Below: Another example of US equipment in Soviet service, this time a M3 Grant tank. Soviet troops called it a 'grave for seven brothers' due to its tendency to burn easily when hit, with fatal results for the crew.

51

Above: Throughout the numerous lines of defence around Kursk, the Soviets dug trenches to accommodate troops, tanks and artillery pieces. Here, Soviet gunners pose for a propaganda photograph.

received numerous support units, including seven independent tank destroyer regiments, and strong artillery support. Vatutin expected the 7th Guards Army, which had a stronger armoured component than 6th Guards Army, to thwart the attack by Army Detachment Kempf. The 1st Tank Army provided the reserve force behind the two guards armies.

Commanded by Lieutenant General M. E. Katukov, the 1st Tank Army consisted of the VI and XXXI Tank and III Mechanised Corps. Also held in reserve was the 69th Army, commanded by Lieutenant General V. D. Kriuchenkin, and the three-division XXXV Guards Rifle Corps. The two formations combined provided a reserve numbering 87,000 men. If necessary, Vatutin could deploy the Stavka's II Guards and V Guards Tank Corps, along with numerous artillery and other support units. Both Rokossovsky in the north and Vatutin in the south concentrated two-thirds of their artillery and tanks in areas where they expected the Germans to attack.

As the main German assault would land on the Kursk salient itself, the Stavka placed Steppe Front, commanded by General Konev, in reserve behind Central and Voronezh fronts. A strong reserve force, Steppe Front contained the 4th and 5th Guards Armies and the 27th, 47th and 53rd Rifle Armies, with a total of 32 rifle divisions. In addition, Steppe Front had the 5th Guards Tank Army, commanded by Lieutenant General Pavel Rotmistrov. Rotmistrov's 5th Guards Tank Army contained the XVIII Tank Corps and XXIX Tank Corps, the III, V, VII and IV Guards Cavalry Corps, the IV Guards Tank Corps and the I, III and V Guards Mechanised Corps. Konev's front, which was further supported by the 5th Air Army, placed a force of 573,195 men, 1639 tanks and self-propelled guns, and 8510 guns and mortars into the field.

The Steppe Front had two important functions. Situated along a line east of Orel to Voronezh, Steppe Front was to prevent the enemy's forces from advancing into the operational and strategic depths that it had accomplished in the past. While part of Konev's force was to fulfil the first role, the remainder was to play an even more important role. The Stavka intended to use the strong arm of Steppe Front to launch its counter-attack. Within five days of the start of Citadel, Soviet commanders would commit Steppe Front to the line opposite the Germans' Army Group South (AGS).

The Germans concentrated AGS in the area near Belgorod. While two major elements would participate in the main attack against Kursk, the Germans held other units in reserve. The Soviets placed Colonel General Rodion Malinovsky's South-western

Front opposite these enemy forces. The 57th Army, 17th Air Army and II Tank Corps formed the Southwestern Front, which had the 5th Air, the 5th Guards Tank and the 47th Armies in reserve. South of Southwestern Front, the Soviets concentrated Army General F. Tolbukhin's Southern Front, which would not play a large role at Kursk.

The most important aspect of the Soviet preparations to meet the impending German offensive at Kursk throughout the spring and early summer of 1943 was the construction of defences. The Soviets began to construct their defences in late March. This gave them three whole months to create an in-depth system of defence. The Soviets wanted to avoid a repeat of previous offensives, when the Germans had easily penetrated their defensive lines. Consequently, the Soviet Army constructed multiple defensive lines around the Kursk salient. Generally, the forces established three 'army' level defence lines, which the units of a particular army manned in the main line of resistance.

In the main line of resistance, the Soviet defences were 3–5km (2–3 miles) deep and contained three to five trench lines with weapons emplacements and

Above: Soviet aircrews prepare captured German SC-250 bombs for use against German airfields and enemy ground troops. It was common practice to write patriotic slogans and insults on them.

Below: A Soviet commissar addresses his troops to give them encouragement on May Day 1943. Even in the middle of a war, Soviet political propaganda managed to find its way to the front.

dugouts. Although the soldiers constructed the first line of 'army' level defence, civilians helped to build the other two. They then constructed three 'front lines' between 15km (9 miles) and 20km (12^1/$_2$ miles) behind the main line of resistance. The front reserves occupied these lines.

Approximately 15km (9 miles) behind the 'front lines', the soldiers and civilians constructed another two or three reserve lines. In the Central Front area alone, the Soviets built more than 5000km (3100 miles) of trenches. They fortified every village and hill and placed more than 400,000 mines in over-grown fields.

Because the Soviets expected the main German thrusts to come in the 13th Army and 48th Army sectors, they installed 112km (70 miles) of barbed wire, 10.7km (6^1/$_2$ miles) of which was electrified, in addition to the standard defences.

Steppe Front established three armies in a screening line in order to prevent the Germans from carrying the offensive east if, by any chance, the

Above: To confuse German pilots flying overhead about the extent of their defences, Soviets placed artillery pieces in entrenched, camouflaged positions. From the air, lowered gun barrels were difficult to spot.

Soviet defences in the bulge failed to contain them. As an added insurance, the Soviets placed one army and two tank armies in reserve to the north-east of Orel. They also positioned one army and one tank army in reserve, this force being stationed east of the Kharkov–Belgorod region.

Below: The German objective in July 1943: the city of Kursk, seen here in February shortly after its recapture by the Red Army. Soviet civilians are detailed to clear away the battle damage.

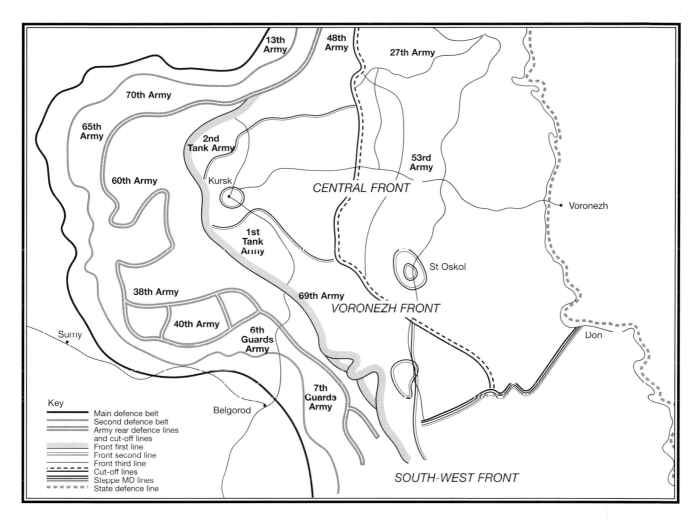

Key
- Main defence belt
- Second defence belt
- Army rear defence lines and cut-off lines
- Front first line
- Front second line
- Front third line
- Cut-off lines
- Steppe MD lines
- State defence line

Above: Deducing that the Germans would attack the Kursk salient, Zhukov and the Stavka commanders ordered the construction of an extensive series of defensive lines around Kursk.

By early July, the Soviets had established a powerful line of anti-tank weapons. First, they built anti-tank minefields to prevent German tanks from reaching the main line of resistance. In the anti-tank gun line, the Soviets created a series of strong points with heavy concentrations of guns in the areas which were most likely to be used by the enemy. They then combined individual strong points into anti-tank areas. In any given battalion-sized anti-tank area, there were at least three company strong points. Each held 4–6 anti-tank guns, 15–20 anti-tank rifles, several tanks and self-propelled guns, and an engineer platoon capable of attacking tanks with mines and grenades. The Soviets used all types of artillery, including anti-aircraft guns, in the anti-tank defences, which were from 30km (18½ miles) to 35km (22 miles) deep. Artillery would play a major defensive role during the battle.

The Soviet defences around Kursk were specifically designed to break up German all-arms teams. Artillery barrages, minefields, pakfronts and machine-gun and sniper nests broke up the German formations. The German *Panzerkeil*, or wedge formation, added to the problem. The German heavy tanks broke through the defences and went on ahead, leaving the less capable tanks at the mercy of the pakfronts, while the infantry were held up by the minefields, artillery bombardments and machine-gun posts. Because Soviet air and ground reconnaissance supplied every single detail of the German preparations, the Stavka could adjust its defences accordingly to the forces attacking each section.

Before the summer of 1943, the Germans had rarely launched a frontal assault against any well-prepared enemy defences. The situation would be different at Kursk. When the Germans did mount a frontal assault against the Soviet's Kursk defences, the outcome would not be what they expected.

CHAPTER FOUR

The Beginning of the Offensive

5 July 1943

After months of preparation, the Germans launched their attack on the Kursk salient. However, the warning given to the Soviets by their intelligence had provided enough time to prepare a suitable welcome.

Initially slated to begin by early May, Operation Citadel, the German attack against the Kursk salient, did not commence as planned. Several factors, including the weather and lack of troop, weapon and equipment reinforcements, caused numerous delays. In addition, Adolf Hitler, who had to give final approval of the plan, seemed unwilling to make a decision. German commanders such as General Heinz Guderian and General Walter Model advised cancellation of the offensive, while the Chief of the Army High Command (OKH) and author of Citadel, Colonel General Kurt Zeitzler, and Field Marshal Günther von Kluge adamantly supported the plan. Despite the debate, the German preparations for the offensive continued. Although Hitler ultimately approved the plan, he later issued a series of delays. Finally, on 1 July, the Führer issued a special order. It explained the purpose of the offensive to all commanders and authorised the start of Citadel, despite the fact that the OKH knew the enemy was aware of the plan.

Throughout the spring and early summer of 1943, the Soviets prepared for the Germans' summer offensive. The

Left: German Junkers Ju87s ('Stukas') in the skies over the Russian front, setting the stage for the opening of Operation Citadel. The Germans intend to achieve rapid breakthroughs with air and artillery supported ground assault.

Above: On 5 July 1943, artillery of the 9th German Army commenced an 80-minute bombardment as a prelude to the ground offensive. The Soviets pre-empted the Germans with one of their own.

Soviets wanted to mask the extent of their preparations and troop strength, as well as their troop movements. Hence they implemented an elaborate tactical, operational and strategic deception plan, or *maskirovka*. Part of the *maskirovka* included the construction of fake trenches and airfields, dummy tanks and artillery, and false tank-dispersal areas. In addition to concealment, the Stavka also clearly assembled troops in some areas to divert German attention from Kursk. The Soviet deception efforts were somewhat successful. German intelligence identified all major enemy units within the Kursk salient, but it did not detect all of the Soviet defensive preparations, especially those within the Steppe Front region. As the Soviets constructed their defences and trained their forces, their intelligence network gathered information about the state of German preparations. Crucial to the Soviets' ability to stop the German advance and to launch their counter-attacks was the determination of exactly where and when the German attack would come; however, Soviet intelligence could not provide that information. Throughout this period of preparation, several false alarms about an impending attack occurred. Consequently, the Stavka issued warnings on at least three separate occasions in May. The uncertainty about when the Germans would attack fuelled the Soviet debate over whether or not to beat the enemy to the punch.

During May, both sides tested the waters. Because they expected the Germans to attack in the near future, Soviet aircraft bombed 17 airfields in the early part of the month. Over the course of three days,

Soviet pilots flew 1400 sorties and destroyed 500 German aircraft at a cost of 122 of their own aircraft. The Germans responded in kind during the second half of the month. German pilots bombed the Kursk railway junction in an attempt to interfere with the enemy's build-up of logistics in the region. Soviet reconnaissance teams and partisans operated behind enemy lines to gather information and disrupt the Germans' logistical build-up. During the month of June, partisans destroyed 298 locomotives, 1222 railroad cars and 44 bridges in the area behind Army Group Centre (AGC).

By the time Hitler issued the orders to begin Operation Citadel, both sides had concentrated a large number of forces. The 9th Army, 4th Panzer Army and Army Detachment Kempf would lead the German assault. The combined strength of these armies was 700,000 men, 2400 tanks and assault guns, and 1800 aircraft. The Soviets' forces on the Central and Voronezh fronts numbered 1.3 million men, 3400 tanks and assault guns, and 2100 aircraft.

Tensions increased as time passed. By 1 July, the Soviet forces were on constant alert. Intelligence indicated an imminent attack, which led the Stavka to warn all commanders that the Germans would launch an assault some time between 3 and 6 July. On 4 July, 100 German aircraft attacked Soviet defences north-west of Belgorod. In addition, enemy

Below: The Soviet barrage caught the Germans by surprise and disrupted their preparations for the offensive. The gun shown below is a Soviet M1937 (ML-20) howitzer firing massive 152mm (6in) shells.

artillery and tanks fired their weapons for several hours. The Soviets responded by implementing the first artillery *kontrpodgotovka*, or disruptive fire, against German positions between Belgorod and Tomarovka with 600 guns and mortars from the 6th Guards Army and 7th Guards Army. Around 1600 hours, German forces facing the southern part of the bulge initiated a reconnaissance-in-force, which was generally a prelude to a major assault. The troops received orders to take out the enemy's command and observation posts, as well as strong points of battalion-size, located in front of the first main defensive line of the Voronezh Front. Furthermore, they were to pinpoint the exact placement of the Soviets' forward defences.

At 2200 hours on 4 July, a Soviet patrol captured a German private, who admitted during questioning that the Germans would attack at dawn the next day. The Soviets contemplated the reliability of this information, which agreed with statements by prisoners during the previous two months. Around 0200 hours on 5 July, Lieutenant General N. P. Pukhov notified Marshal Georgi Zhukov of the capture of a German combat engineer from the 6th Infantry Division, who had been clearing a path through the minefields in preparation for the offensive, which he predicted would commence at 0300 hours. After careful consideration, Zhukov, as Deputy Commander of the Soviet Army and the Stavka representative for the northern region of the Kursk bulge, ordered an alert. In turn, General Konstantin Rokossovsky, the commander of Central Front, decided to begin the planned counter-preparation artillery barrage immediately. By 0220 hours on 5 July, the Central Front went into action.

The guns of the 13th Army opened fire against German artillery batteries and infantry and tank assembly areas. In addition to causing numerous casualties, Soviet shells succeeded in destroying some of the Germans' artillery positions and in cutting telephone lines. An hour after Central Front began its artillery barrage, the 6th Guards Army, in the Voronezh Front, began a second *kontrpodgotovka*. The Soviet counter-preparation achieved mixed results. Bombardment against known German artillery positions had a devastating effect and caught German gunners in the open as they were preparing to fire their own artillery barrage. Shells falling in areas where the German positions remained unknown frequently failed to cause much damage.

Above: Von Kluge (left) and Model (right), the commander of 9th Army, discuss the initial progress of the German attack. The initial breakthrough the Germans had hoped for did not prove forthcoming.

The Soviet counter-preparation bombardments did, however, force the German Army High Command (OKH) to delay AGC's opening actions for more than two hours and that of Army Group South (AGS) for almost three hours.

Even as Soviet artillery opened its attack in the early morning hours of 5 July, the Soviet Air Force attempted to catch the Luftwaffe's aircraft on the ground. German radar warned of the approaching enemy aircraft. The Soviet Air Force suffered heavy losses and failed to knock out the Luftwaffe and its bases. Consequently, German aircraft were able to provide the initial ground attacks with the necessary air support.

Before dawn on 5 July, the German summer offensive began. At 0430 hours, after the completion of Central Front's counter-preparation barrage, the 9th German Army commenced its own artillery bombardment, which lasted for 80 minutes. General

CHAPTER FIVE

Model's Main Effort
Northern Thrust

Never a keen supporter of Operation Citadel, Model nonetheless struggled to implement the Führer's wishes. Unfortunately for him, his units faced determined Soviet opposition, and a breakthrough was to prove elusive.

During the spring and early summer of 1943, the Soviets constructed an extensive defensive network of trenches and strongholds in and behind the Kursk salient. A plateau called the Central Russian Uplands dominated the terrain in the northern part of the bulge between Orel and Kursk, in the Central Front sector. While the Germans concentrated their forces around Orel in the north, the Soviets controlled the southern part of the plateau. The Soviet Army constructed a series of defensive lines from the northern edge of the salient along the ridge north of the Svapa River valley to the area north of Kursk along the Oka River. A number of small streams facilitated the Soviet defences. Although they were generally dry during the month of July, summer thunderstorms frequently filled them with water temporarily. The prize at the centre of the salient behind the myriad Soviet defences was Kursk, an important rail and road centre. Control of Kursk was crucial to the defence of the bulge itself. While the Germans were determined to capture the city and sever Soviet communications, the Soviets were equally resolved to keep Kursk out of the hands of their German enemies.

Left: German graves in Maloarkhangel'sk. From the start, both sides suffered heavy casualties, and while much of the fighting occured in open countryside, nearby towns and villages suffered as well.

On 5 July, the 9th German Army, commanded by General Walter Model, launched a major attack against the Central Front's 13th Army. Trained in anti-tank tactics, Soviet infantrymen did not panic when confronted by Tiger and Ferdinand tanks. They gave ground grudgingly and made the enemy's advances costly. The fierce level of fighting, witnessed on the first day of Citadel as the two armies clashed, would continue for days and would grind down both the attackers and the defenders. As both the Germans and the Soviets were equally determined to accomplish their goals, the campaign developed into a battle of attrition.

The Soviets, who could continue an attritional conflict much longer than their opponent, wanted to drain the Germans' strength before launching their planned counter-offensive. Despite warnings to the contrary from Model, Colonel General Heinz Guderian and other German commanders, neither Adolf Hitler nor the operation's supporters envisioned what the exact cost of Operation Citadel ultimately would be.

Above: Pleased with the Central Front's defence during the battle's first days, General Rokossovsky meets his men. A proponent of mobile warfare, he was confident after his success at Stalingrad.

According to the German plan, Model's 9th Army would break through the Soviet defences, advance southwards to Kursk and link up with the northward-moving 4th Panzer Army. Once the two armies had joined and cut off the Soviet troops within the salient, they could systematically destroy the enemy. Josef Stalin and the Supreme High Command (Stavka) fully intended to prevent the Germans accomplishing their goal and launching another major offensive in the Soviet Union. As commander of Central Front, Colonel General Konstantin Rokossovsky was resolved to use his 13th Army and other formations to thwart the German plan. After stopping the 9th Army's attack, Rokossovsky intended to launch a counter-attack to destroy the enemy.

By the end of the first day of the campaign, the Germans had broken through the first line of Soviet defences and created a gap in the line that was 15km

(9$\frac{1}{4}$ miles) wide and 8km (5 miles) deep. Both the Germans and the Soviets had suffered heavy losses in men, tanks and other equipment. Late on 5 July, Rokossovsky reported the results of the first day of battle and discussed his options with Josef Stalin. Recognising that the enemy would renew its offensive the next day, Rokossovsky wanted to mount a counter-attack to stop it. Initially, Stalin promised to transfer Lieutenant General S. G. Trofimenko's 27th Army to Rokossovsky's command. A short time later, however, because of the dire situation on the Voronezh Front, Stalin modified his orders. They now stated that Rokossovsky could no longer rely upon reinforcement from the 27th Army. The Central Front commander chose to launch a counter-attack regardless, even though he did not receive the additional troops and tanks from Stalin. However, Rokossovsky did order formations such as the XIX and III Tank Corps to proceed to the front. The two tank corps would assist the counter-attack launched by elements of the 13th, 48th and 70th Armies with the support of the 2nd Tank Army.

At 0350 hours on 6 July, the IV Artillery Penetration Corps opened a barrage aimed at the Germans' front lines. Ten minutes later, Soviet dive-bombers arrived to attack the enemy's tanks and infantry. A short time later, German fighters appeared in the skies and an intense air battle commenced. As the battle raged overhead, the Soviet assault began. At dawn, despite the fact that the XIX and III Tank Corps had not yet reached their positions, XVII Guards Corps and the 2nd Tank Army's XVI Tank Corps attacked. As the battle began, the

scene recalled visions of the previous world war. Burning cornfields and thatched roofs created smoke, which drifted over trenches and barbed wire. Oily, black clouds rose from smouldering tanks that had been destroyed on the first day. Thundering Soviet artillery guns drowned out the noise of small arms and machine-gun fire.

As soon as it arrived, the XIX Tank Corps moved forwards through the 132nd and 175th Soviet Rifle Divisions to attack the XXXXVI German Panzer Corps. After initial Soviet success, 250 German tanks, followed by infantry, pushed back the attacking units. Enemy tanks also stopped a three-division counter-attack, ordered by Lieutenant General N. P. Pukhov, the commander of 13th Army. In order to meet the threat of the Soviet counter-attack and to continue their own offensive, the Germans committed the 2nd and 9th Panzer Divisions and the 505th Tiger Division to the battle. Concentrated in the area between Ponyri and Soborovka, the main German tank force possessed more than 1000 tanks, 3000 guns and mortars, and 5000 machine guns. Confronted by a huge armoured force that threatened to roll back the Soviet defenders, Rokossovsky ordered the 60th Army, commanded by Lieutenant General I. D. Cherniakhovsky, to move to the front lines. While one of Cherniakhovsky's divisions rapidly moved up, Lieutenant General P. I. Batov ordered two of 65th Army's tank regiments to the front.

Below: Billowing smoke rises from burning tanks on a large plain, evidence of the fierce battle that will rage for days. In the foreground are a PzKpfw IV (left) and a PzKpfw III (right).

Fierce fighting raged along Rokossovsky's front line throughout the day. After it repelled attacks by the XVI Tank Corps, two German panzer divisions, with approximately 300 tanks, attacked the XVII Guards Rifle Corps as they advanced towards Ol'khovatka and Ponyri. Although initially the Soviets withstood the assault, the Germans brought up additional infantry and tanks, and forced the corps to withdraw to the 13th Army's second line of defences. Lieutenant General A.G. Rodin's 2nd Tank Army failed to make much headway in its attack against German armoured formations; however, the German advance slowed significantly as it reached the 13th Army's main defences. Both the Soviet and German commanders used the night of 6 July to evaluate the situation, as well as to make preparations for the next day's combat. Anticipating another German attack with heavy tanks, Rokossovsky decided to shift his tank units to the defensive. This

Below: Two German soldiers, laden down with equipment and ammunition, work their way through the debris-littered battlefield towards a disabled T-34 tank during the fighting.

meant that the troops had to dig trenches in which to bury the tanks, leaving only their turrets above ground level. Rokossovsky also ordered his subordinates to launch counter-attacks against the enemy's light tanks and infantry only.

When the fighting ended on 6 July, the Soviet tanks were maintaining a defensive position against a total of nine German divisions: six infantry and three panzer. Soviet units had to be prepared to withstand an attack by an even larger German force. The Central Front commander moved reinforcements into the region around Ponyri, and he transferred the 81st Rifle Division from the reserve area to a defensive position behind the XVII Guards Rifle Corps, which also received reinforcement from the 43rd and 58th tank regiments. In addition to preparing his defences, Rokossovsky also intended to launch further counter-attacks. He ordered the III Soviet Tank Corps to attack the enemy at Ponyri and the XVIII Guards Rifle Corps to push back the Germans' 78th Sturm Infantry Division.

The Soviet counter-attack of 6 July had prevented Model's 9th Army from making as much progress in

the northern sector of the salient as Adolf Hitler had demanded. Model, therefore, decided to amass an even larger armoured force and attack the centre of the Soviet line. Consequently, he decided to commit units being held in reserve for the drive on Kursk after the breakthrough. He therefore ordered XXXXI Panzer Corps' 18th Panzer Division, one of the units held in reserve, to be prepared to launch an attack with its 200 tanks. The XXXXVII Panzer Corps' 4th Panzer Division had already begun its move to the front line. In addition, Model ordered the 12th Panzer, the 10th Panzergrenadier and the 36th Motorised Divisions, which were situated south of Orel, to be prepared to enter the battle. When they renewed the offensive on 7 July, the Germans hoped to penetrate the second line of Soviet defences. Because of the strength of the 13th Soviet Army's defences and of the tank-supported counter-attacks of the previous day, Model set more conservative goals for the next phase of the offensive. What the German commander failed to realise, however, was that Rokossovsky had concentrated more than 3000 guns and mortars, 5000 machine guns, and 1000 tanks in the centre of his line.

The attacks begun by Model's 9th Army at dawn on 7 July initiated a day of extremely fierce fighting, as the Germans strove to pierce the 13th Army's second defensive line. With help from XXXXI Panzer

Above: Dawn, 5 July 1943. A German '88' (88mm (3.45in)) gun opens up on Soviet positions during the opening bombardment of the offensive. The '88' was a highly-effective tank killer.

Corps divisions, the XXXXVII Panzer Corps began the attack. Model threw more than 400 tanks and 4 infantry divisions along the railroad line between Ponyri and Ol'khovatka, which was 10km (6 miles) to the west. The 18th Panzer Division and 9th Panzer Division spearheaded the assault. While the 2nd Panzer Division and 20th Panzer Division attacked west towards Samodurovka-Molotych, other formations moved towards Ponyri. In Model's initial assault, 10 infantry and 4 panzer divisions hit the Soviet defences. During the night, however, additional Soviet formations – the 11th Mortar and 46th Light Artillery brigades and the 12th Artillery Regiment – had moved forwards into the area near Ponyri to strengthen the defences.

Both the Germans and the Soviets believed that control of Ponyri was crucial because of its position at a major railway junction between Orel and Kursk. The most intense fighting between the 9th German Army and the 13th Soviet Army occurred over Ponyri. Two divisions of the XXXXI Panzer Corps – the 18th Panzer and the 292nd Infantry Divisions – attacked Ponyri five times. The 307th Rifle Division, commanded by Major General M.A. Enshin, repelled

Above: A German officer confers with two military policemen near the town of Podolyan on 6 July 1943. Military police controlled the flow of traffic carrying reinforcements or equipment behind the front lines.

the Germans each time. Numerous tank casualties resulted from mines and heavy artillery-fire. Soviet rifle-fire cut down enemy infantrymen as they attempted to work their way around the burning tanks and through the barbed wire and other obstacles that were surrounding the city. When German tank-supported infantry reached the north-western outskirts of Ponyri, a counter-attack by the 307th

Rifle Division forced them to retreat. The Germans launched numerous attacks against the town and the surrounding areas. Late in the afternoon, the Germans attacked the town from three sides: the north, east and west. Still the Soviets held on. As the battle raged, the Germans brought up fresh troops. General Pukhov rushed reinforcements to the region. At 1900 hours, an additional German 60 tanks and 2 more infantry units entered the fray. The intensity of the enemy attack finally forced the 307th Rifle Division to withdraw to the southern part of Ponyri. The Germans continued to apply pressure on the Soviet defenders. By the end of the day, the Germans, who had suffered heavy losses, only controlled half of Ponyri.

Even as the battle for Ponyri raged, the XXXXVII Panzer Corps' 2nd and 20th Panzer Divisions advanced southwards towards Ol'khovatka. In some respects, Model thought that it was more important to control this village than Ponyri. Key to Ol'khovatka's importance was its high ground, in particular Hill 274. The hills of Ol'khovatka formed the centre of the Central Russian ridge that extended

Left: The battle raging around them, a Soviet anti-tank rifle team move forward. With battle taking place at such short ranges, even the puny anti-tank rifle could penetrate German armour.

from Orel to Belgorod. Model believed that this was the doorway to Kursk, which lay south of Ol'khovatka. After seizing the high ground, the German commander planned to move up his reserves to exploit his success. Model could then engage Rokossovsky's forces, especially his armoured formations, in an area in which they had a territorial disadvantage. Model believed that this disadvantage would facilitate the Soviets' defeat and enable his advance to Kursk, where he expected to meet the 4th Panzer Army.

Anticipating such a move, Rokossovsky had transferred two of Rodin's 2nd Tank Army corps – the XVI and XIX Tank Corps – to the Ol'khovatka sector on the night of 6 July. At the same time, he ordered the 3rd Destroyer Brigade to the area. The results of the tank corps' counter-attacks were not decisive; however, the combined firepower from the tanks and two guards rifle divisions caused heavy losses to the 2nd Panzer Division and 20th Panzer Division tanks. By mid-afternoon, supported by the 505th Tiger Detachment and the 20th Panzer Division, the 2nd Panzer Division, with its 140 tanks and 50 assault

guns, launched another thrust against the Soviet defences between Samodurovka and Ol'khovatka, but the Germans failed to penetrate them. Throughout the day, the fighting around Samodurovka and Ol'khovatka was intense. Smoke from burning tanks filled the air, as the deafening noise of the battle increased. Continuous attacks and counter-attacks characterised the fierceness of the struggle as both sides vied for victory.

Situated on the right flank opposite the Soviet 70th Army, the XXXXVI Panzer Corps achieved similar results when it came in contact with Soviet defences. Two of the corps' infantry divisions fought the 280th Soviet Rifle Division for the high ground in the Soloschonki area. Although the German divisions took a hill, the Soviets quickly regained possession of it. Both sides moved up reinforcements. Despite repeated attacks against the reinforced 280th Soviet Rifle Division, the Germans failed to widen the base

Below: Horribly exposed to enemy fire, a German soldier races for cover through the stark, open countryside and past fallen trees, carrying a heavy load of fresh machine gun ammunition.

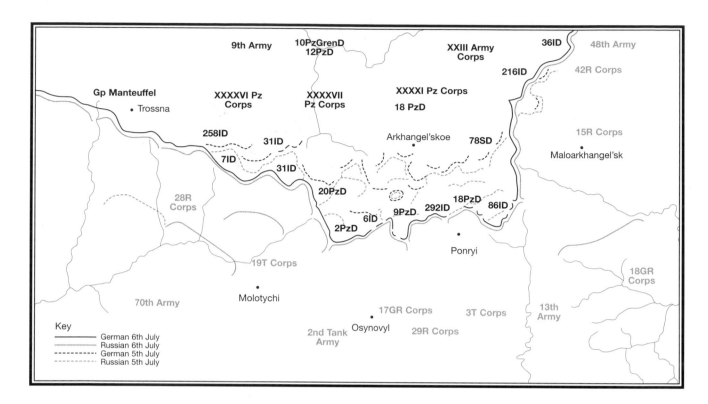

Above: During the first days of Citadel, the 9th German Army made small gains against the Central Front defenders. In fact, as the struggle went on, German gains decreased, while their losses increased.

of their overall attack. By the end of the day, the XXXXVI Panzer Corps were not much better off and had made little progress.

Along a 32km (20 mile) front, elements of Rodin's 2nd Tank Army and Pukhov's 13th Army had engaged seven German infantry and four panzer divisions in battle. Between the villages of Saborovka and Ponyri, a huge tank battle would begin and rage for four days. At its peak, more than 2000 tanks would participate in a slogging match over the high ground at the heart of the Soviet Central Front defences. The fierce battle raged unabated all along the front throughout the day. On the east flank of the 9th Army, the 74th Soviet Rifle Division attacked the 78th German Sturm Infantry Division 11 times. The German infantrymen withstood each assault, but it became increasingly difficult for them to do so. In support of the attacks, the 12th Soviet Artillery Division concentrated an intense artillery barrage against the enemy division. As the 78th Sturm Infantry Division's position weakened, a company of Ferdinand tank destroyers arrived to bolster it. Despite the strength of the Soviet attack, the German division did not retreat.

The 9th Army made small gains on 7 July, but, overall, its efforts failed to accomplish much. Even with heavy armoured attacks, the Germans could not penetrate the Soviet defences, which were backed by large artillery formations. As the Soviet anti-tank guns inflicted heavy damage on the advancing enemy tanks, the panzer divisions received few replacement tanks. Also, although the 9th Army suffered 10,000 casualties during the first three days of fighting, only 5000 replacements arrived in the front line. German ground troops did not have the air support that they had enjoyed during the first two days of the campaign. Beginning on 7 July, the Central Front's Air Force successfully implemented its air plan. Large groups of fighters patrolled the battlefield and responded to requests for support. As more Soviet aircraft entered the skies over the Central Front's battlefield, German aircraft losses increased. The number of Soviet sorties increased and the Soviet air forces achieved general air superiority.

As a result of the poor performance by the Luftwaffe and the lack of tank- and manpower replacements, the Germans' ability to continue to make progress was greatly limited. Despite the situation, Model planned to attack again the next day. During the night, the 9th Army brought up reinforcements. More than 400 tanks and two infantry divisions moved into the areas around Snova,

Podsoborovka and Saborovka, three villages west of Ponyri. The Soviets, however, also brought up reinforcements, particularly around Ponyri. Lieutenant General I.V. Galanin, the commander of the 70th Army, transferred the 140th and 162nd Rifle Divisions to Teploe, where they were to remain in reserve until needed against the main German attack. Galanin also ordered the 181st Rifle Division to move closer to the attack zone and the 229th and 259th tank regiments to provide reinforcement for 13th Army.

On 8 July, although the Germans renewed their offensive, the Soviets ultimately grabbed the initiative on the battlefield. At times, however, the struggle in both important sectors of the Central Front reached the critical stage. Before the XXXXVII Panzer Corps' ground attack began, the Germans' guns shelled the Soviet front lines. At 0800 hours, General Dietrich von Saucken's 4th Panzer Division added 101 tanks to the battle when it joined the 20th

Panzer Division in the fight for Samodurovka. At the same time, the 2nd Panzer Division, commanded by General Vollrath von Lubbe, threw its 118 tanks against the Soviet defences at Ol'khovatka. The 20th Panzer Division opened the road to Teploe. Saucken ordered his 4th Panzer Division to Teploe and Hill 272. German Stukas, providing support for the advancing tanks and infantry, bombed Soviet artillery positions. The Soviet anti-tank units remained within their protected trenches as they waited for the bombardment to end and the ground attack to begin. Black smoke and dust filled the air. The noise was deafening. Ju 87s also attacked the entrenched enemy forces. As Henschel Hs129 ground-attack aircraft searched for concentrations of troops and armour, Focke-Wulf FW 190 fighters

Below: A German soldier takes advantage of a lull in the fighting to relax and smoke a cigarette; his battle-weary comrade has no energy to do anything other than stare vacantly ahead.

protected them. The onslaught of bad weather, however, prevented the Luftwaffe from maintaining its protection of the ground forces throughout the day.

When the ground assault began, the German forces met stiff resistance. During the night, Rokossovsky had brought up two rifle divisions, an artillery division, two armoured brigades and a mechanised rifle brigade to provide additional protection for Teploe. As a battalion of the 33rd Panzergrenadier Regiment led the assault, Soviet artillery and machine-gun fire cut down at least 100 enemy soldiers. Despite the casualties, the German advance continued and forced the Soviet defenders out of Teploe. The Soviets retreated a short distance and regrouped on Hill 272, the last bit of high ground near the village. Saucken immediately ordered the 3rd and 35th panzer regiments to attack. He wanted to prevent the Soviets organising a new defensive position or counterattacking.

Unknown to Saucken, Colonel V.N. Rukosuyev had deployed his 3rd Anti-Tank Artillery Brigade into camouflaged positions on the hill. Entrenched T-34s provided support for the brigade. Infantrymen, equipped with anti-tank rifles that could damage tanks at close range, covered the T-34s' flanks. When the Germans' forward elements attacked, the entrenched Soviets opened fire. The combined efforts of the Luftwaffe and the tank attack quickly

Below: A pair of PzKpfw VI Tiger tanks emerge out of the smoke on the battlefield. They have knocked out two T-34 tanks, and the lead Tiger has just fired its gun at another target.

resulted in the destruction of at least one Soviet battery. A direct hit from a bomb took out the battery's last gun and its crew. Some of the most brutal fighting of the first few days occurred during the 48 hours during which control of Hill 272 was contested. The Germans captured the hill twice, but each time the defenders counterattacked and drove them back. A battalion of the 33rd Panzergrenadier Regiment led the third, and final, German attack on Hill 272. Although they recaptured the hill, the Germans lost it again to a Soviet counter-thrust. When the dust cleared, the 3rd Anti-Tank Artillery Brigade effectively no longer existed.

In an attempt to breach the ridge defensive line between the Soviets' 70th and 13th Armies, the 4th Panzer Division and 20th Panzer Division hit the enemy four times. The brunt of the attack fell on the XVII Guards Rifle Corps. German tanks, supported by infantry, attacked Samodurovka, Hill 257 and the ridge north of Ol'khovatka in waves of 60–100 tanks. Hill 257, which housed the defensive centre of XVII Guards Rifle Corps, became the site of the fiercest fighting on 8 July. Although the Germans succeeded in occupying Hill 257 by 1700 hours, they made little progress elsewhere against the XVII Guards Rifle Corps' defences. Repeated attempts to drive the Soviets out of Samodurovka and Ol'khovatka failed.

As the 20th Panzer Division continued its assault on Samodurovka, the 4th Panzer Division, with its tanks and assault guns leading the way, forced its way through the area where the defences of the 175th Guards Rifle Division and 70th Guards Rifle

Division came together. The village of Teploe fell to the Germans. Rokossovsky and Pukhov immediately ordered the 140th Rifle Division and a 2nd Tank Army reserve brigade, the 11th Guards Tank Brigade, to close the hole in the line. As these units moved forwards, the Soviets continued to hold the ridge south of the village. The fighting intensified. Repeated German efforts failed to force the defenders to relinquish their control of the ridge.

As the defenders of Teploe retreated, Soviet troops around Ponyri held their positions. Although their pressure against the 6th Guards Rifle Division, situated west of Ponyri, resulted in minor gains, the Germans failed to cross the Ponyri–Ol'khovatka road, which was only a short distance from their starting point. The tanks of the XVI Tank Corps and XIX Tank Corps, in conjunction with the firepower from anti-tank guns and artillery, mounted a stiff defence against the German advance. Launching a series of counter-attacks, the two tank corps stopped the German advance shortly after it began. During the day, further reinforcements – the 11th Guards and 129th Tank brigades and the 4th Guards Parachute Division – arrived to bolster the Soviet defensive effort.

Right: With the road open before it, a column of US-supplied light tanks rush forwards. As the battle intensified, both the German and the Soviet commanders ordered their tank reserves to the front lines.

Above: Ordered to plug a hole in the line, Soviet soldiers catch a ride to the front. Quick reactions by Soviet riflemen and tank crews were to prevent a rapid German breakthrough at Kursk.

Further to the east, the battle for Ponyri continued on 8 July. The 307th Rifle Division consolidated its forces during the night and at dawn counterattacked across a field littered with dead Soviet and German soldiers and still-smouldering tanks and artillery pieces. The 307th Rifle Division recaptured the northern part of Ponyri, but the struggle for control

would continue unabated for the next two days. On several occasions, both Model and Pukhov committed new troops to the battle. However, at the end of the day, both the Germans and the Soviets controlled part of the town.

As the German efforts faltered on 8 July, Model met with his corps commanders to assess the situation. The Germans had failed to accomplish a quick tank-supported breakthrough because the Soviets had laid extensive minefields and constructed heavy defences. Although he had not strongly believed that a quick breakthrough to Kursk by the 9th Army was possible, Model now considered it impossible. Four days of brutal fighting had caused tens of thousands of human, as well as a large number of tank, casualties. Unless new tactics were devised, it would take another four to five days of attritional fighting to break the Soviet defences. To implement new tactics,

Below: A Soviet aircrew prepares for a mission. By 1943, the Soviet Air Force was better equipped than it was in 1941, bombing German airfields and providing support for the troops on the ground.

however, he would need even greater resources of men, tanks, materiel and munitions. At the end of the day, Model reported the situation to Army Group Centre (AGC) commander, Field Marshal Günther von Kluge. Four days of intense fighting had taken a toll on the infantry and panzer units. Although the Luftwaffe had mounted valiant efforts to support the offensive, fuel shortages limited its ability to continue. Kluge expected the 9th Army to resume the offensive the next day; therefore, Model reluctantly regrouped his forces and issued attack orders. The 9th Army commander planned one last effort to take Ol'khovatka. The blood of the corpses from the previous attempts had soaked the ground around the village. The capture of Ol'khovatka might vindicate their wasted lives.

The XXXXVII Panzer Corps received orders to resume the assault on 9 July. German Stuka dive-bombers and artillery fire would ready the field for a new day of fighting. Five divisions – the 20th, 4th, 2nd and 9th Panzer Divisions and the 6th Infantry Division – would again lead the attack in an effort to

Above: During World War II, the Ilyushin Il-2 was the backbone of Soviet ground-attack units. Heavy armour and sturdy construction made it resistant to damage and its armament was deadly to tanks.

penetrate the Soviet defensive line. Lieutenant General Joachim Lemelsen, the commander of XXXXVII Panzer Corps, created the Panzer Brigade Burmeister from tank battalions of the 2nd and 4th Panzer Divisions. The German formations moved into position during the night and prepared for the next day's assault. Lemelsen concentrated his 300 tanks at the head of the assault force. Infantry support would follow.

Early on 9 July, the German Stukas and artillery did their job, as the XXXXVII Panzer Corps divisions prepared to strike. A devastating bombardment hit the Soviet defences, but it would not be enough. A short time later, the newly formed Panzer Brigade Burmeister advanced towards Samodurovka. After the attackers captured a hill south of Samodurovka, fire from Soviet anti-tank weapons prevented the further advance of the brigade. The 2nd Panzer, 9th Panzer and 6th Infantry Divisions tangled with the Soviets along the Ponyri–Ol'khovatka road and the German advance slowed. The Soviets moved up heavy artillery from the south, as well as the 162nd Rifle Division of the 70th Army, to meet the enemy tank threat. The XXXXVII Panzer Corps attacks had little effect on the Soviet defences and the corps' advance ground to a halt. At 2200 hours on 9 July, the Soviet 6th Guards Rifle Division launched a counter-attack against the 9th Panzer Division in the area west of Ol'khovatka.

The Soviets took the initiative in other areas along the front. After attacking the XXXXVI Panzer Corps

area with artillery fire, 70th Army formations mounted a minor assault against the 20th Panzer Division. General Zorn, commander of XXXXIV Panzer Corps, joined the 31st Infantry and the 20th Panzer Divisions together to form Group Esebeck. Deploying it to the junction of XXXXVI Panzer Corps and XXXXVII Panzer Corps, Zorn ordered Group Esebeck to attack. Although it made a small break in the Soviet defences at Samodurovka, the 20th Panzer Division failed to exploit the penetration. The division did, however, manage to maintain control of some high ground south of Samodurovka. The other XXXXVI Panzer Corps divisions remained on the defensive because of heavy Soviet assaults.

Not all of the Germans' panzer corps maintained defensive positions. XXXXI Panzer Corps formations did resume the offensive. At 0630 hours on 9 July, the 18th Panzer Division and the 292nd Infantry Division renewed the attack on Ponyri. Despite strong resistance, the divisions made a 500m (547yd) hole in the Soviet line. Heavy fighting continued into the afternoon, as Soviet artillery-supported tank counter-attacks attempted, but failed, to close the hole in the defences.

In addition to meeting the German assaults of 9 July, Soviet forces responded with their own. Situated on the 9th Army's left flank, the XXIII Army

Left: A German command post hidden in a small wood from any danger of Soviet air attack. A field telephone handset hangs from the trunk of a tree for communicating with the front lines.

Corps came under attack. As well as a ground assault against the 78th Sturm Infantry Division, the Soviets also gathered their forces in order to rain a heavy artillery bombardment on both the 78th Sturm and the 216th Infantry Divisions. The Soviet attack against the XXIII Army Corps and XXXXI Panzer Corps would continue into the evening of 9 July, and the XXXXVII Panzer Corps and XXXXVI Panzer Corps could do nothing but maintain defensive positions as 9 July drew to a close.

Several factors indicated that Model's 9th Army had little chance of reaching Kursk as 10 July neared. First, 9th Army had suffered heavy casualties in men and machines during the five days of fighting. Losses already outnumbered replacements. Germany's ability to provide a continuous flow of human and materiel reinforcement for an extended period of time was questionable. Secondly, during the afternoon of 9 July, Model ordered a cessation of the attack in order to allow his troops to rest and his tanks to be repaired. The 9th Army was exhausted. Model did not have confidence in his force's capacity for continuing the fight indefinitely. Thirdly, the offensive had deteriorated into an attritional battle, which Germany did not necessarily have the resources either to maintain or to win. Finally, despite the continued commitment of formations, German advances against the Soviets' Central Front defences had progressively declined. Although he knew before the start of the offensive that the Soviets

Below: Soviet reserves march to the front. By 9 July, both sides were rushing reinforcements to the front, the Germans determined to achieve a major breakthrough, the Soviets just as committed to preventing one.

had constructed an extensive network of defensive strongholds and trenches, the 9th Army commander had no concept of what the cost of repeated frontal assaults against the entrenched enemy would be. Model informed Field Marshal von Kluge that a 9th Army breakthrough to Kursk was now no longer a realistic expectation. Kluge was not necessarily ready to accept Model's opinion.

The poor results of 9 July indicated the uphill battle that the Germans faced as the campaign continued, but continue it did. Although he had not given the offensive enthusiastic support at the beginning, Hitler was not ready to call it quits, and he refused to allow Model to authorise a retreat. Understanding the reality of the situation, Model's objectives for 10 July were modest. The German commander did not set unrealistic goals and the fierce, in some cases almost desperate, fighting

Above: Soldiers take a break from the heavy fighting. The soldiers' posture indicates that they do not fear an imminent enemy attack. Behind them a Tiger's tank crew rest with their vehicle under a tree.

resumed in the early morning hours of 10 July. Maintaining the defensive on the XXIII Army Corps and XXXXI Panzer Corps fronts, Model ordered a concentrated effort by XXXXVI Panzer Corps and XXXXVII Panzer Corps against the Soviet defences near Teploe and against the flank of the 70th Soviet Army. Because it possessed the majority of 9th Army's tanks, XXXXVII Panzer Corps received orders to advance southwards 5km (3 miles) to take the high ground near Molotychi.

Although there was now little hope of achieving success, the XXXXVI Panzer Corps and XXXXVII Panzer Corps began their preparations to renew the attack the next day.

87

CHAPTER SIX

Southern Thrust

A Hard Struggle

In the south, the German offensive was faring somewhat better, but still Manstein could not achieve the breakthrough he wanted. Both sides piled reinforcements into the battle in an attempt to gain a decisive advantage.

Although the German thrust against the northern face of the Kursk bulge did not proceed as planned, German forces moving north from Belgorod were able to make greater headway than those moving south from Orel. As the campaign between the Germans' Army Group South (AGS) and the Soviets' Voronezh Front developed, the two sides threw more than 4000 tanks, 7000 guns and mortars, and almost 2000 aircraft into the battle. As was the case in the northern part of the salient, the fighting in the southern part was extremely intense. Despite fierce Soviet resistance, determined German forces advanced 35km (21³/₄ miles) before being stopped by the 1st Soviet Tank Army. However, the attackers did not come close to breaking out or even to encircling the Soviet defenders.

During the afternoon of 4 July, the Germans initiated small assaults against some of Voronezh Front's combat security strong points and advanced to the forward edge of the Soviet's main line of resistance (MLR). After dark, the Germans carried out reconnaissance near the 7th Guards Army's front. The commander of the Voronezh Front area, Army General Nikolai Vatutin, deployed the

Left: German soldiers advance on 7 July to secure the front line near Soborovka. The 4th Panzer Army fared much better in the south than the 9th Army did in the north, but still failed to meet its objectives for the first day.

6th Guards Army to man the front near Belgorod. The 7th Guards Army provided protection for the 6th Guards Army's left flank. Shortly before the German offensive got underway, in the early morning hours of 5 July, a Soviet artillery bombardment against the enemy's front line began. The Soviet artillery fire caused a delay in the commencement of the ground operation against Voronezh Front by Colonel General Hermann Hoth's 4th Panzer Army. Before first light, however, German aircraft and artillery began the assault on Vatutin's front lines. As the 4th Panzer Army attacked from west of the Donetz River, Army Detachment Kempf hit the Soviet Army from the river's east.

Hoth arranged his troops into a powerful wedge for the attack. The Tiger and other heavy tanks formed the first wall. Behind these tanks came the older medium tanks, followed by the infantry. The XXXXVIII Panzer Corps and II SS Panzer Corps spearheaded Hoth's attack towards Kursk on the roads through Prokhorovka and Oboian. Led by Tiger tanks, the two corps launched a heavy thrust against General I. M. Chistiakov's 6th Guards Army sector. Although not surprised by the enemy attack,

Below: Attacks by XXXXVII Panzer Corps and II SS Panzer Corps pierced the Soviets' first line of defence in the south. Vatutin reinforced the 7th Guards Army and the 40th Army to meet the threat.

the defenders had a difficult time trying to stop the enemy. The 67th Guards Rifle Division and 52nd Guards Rifle Division bore the brunt of the assault. Within a couple of hours, two divisions of XXXXVIII Panzer Corps – the 3rd Panzer and *Grossdeutschland* Divisions – pierced the 67th Guards Rifle Division's first line of defence. As the panzer corps' divisions passed through the break in the line, Soviet artillery guns opened up and forced the tanks to seek cover. A sudden but brief thunderstorm flooded several gullies, which also served to hinder the advance of XXXXVIII Panzer Corps.

A Soviet counter-attack failed to stem the powerful German panzer corps. Despite the beating that it took from the Soviet artillery and the thunderstorm, Hoth's 4th Panzer Army continued to push against the Soviet defenders. Vatutin committed Lieutenant General M. E. Katukov's 1st Tank Army and the II Guards Indendent Corps and V Guards Independent Corps, which were part of Voronezh Front's reserves, into the army's second line of defence. The Soviet commander also ordered these units to launch attacks to stop the enemy.

The 52nd Guards Rifle Division found itself under attack from elements of both the XXXXVIII Panzer Corps and the II SS Panzer Corps, something which it could not withstand. Three SS panzergrenadier divisions, supported by an infantry division,

Above: Soviet prisoners wait to be taken to the rear while the crews of a platoon of Panthers check over their vehicles during a lull in the fighting. The gun barrel cover suggests they are not close to the front.

punched their way through the 52nd Guards Rifle Division's anti-tank defences as they moved to the north towards Bykovka. Two anti-tank regiments inflicted damage on the enemy's tanks as they attempted to stop them. The intense fighting took its toll on both sides, but the penetration of the Soviet lines by the II SS Panzer Corps continued. Although it suffered almost 30 per cent casualties, the 52nd Guards Rifle Division refused to give up the fight. By early evening, the II SS Panzer Corps had advanced almost 20km (12 miles) deep into the minefields and obstacles protecting the second line of 6th Guards Army's defences.

Throughout the day, the German panzer corps pounded away at the Soviet defences. By the day's end, the divisions of 6th Guards Army withdrew from their positions along the Cherkasskoe axis and occupied the next line of defences. While the 6th Guards Army tried to stop Hoth's advancing 4th Panzer Army, Army Detachment Kempf, commanded by General Werner Kempf, moved against Lieutenant General M.S. Shumilov's 7th Guards Army. Five divisions began to cross the Northern Donetz River and attack the Soviet army's main line of resistance. Some, but not all, of the Germans' attempts at getting over the river succeeded. Despite strong Soviet resistance, German troops captured a bridgehead on the river's eastern bank. Approximately 10–12km

(6–7½ miles) wide and 3–4km (2–2½ miles) deep, the bridgehead formed a wedge in the 7th Guards Army's main line of defence.

The situation on the Voronezh Front did not look good; however, the Soviet commanders rose to the challenge and began to send reinforcements to support the 6th Guards Army. Although Vatutin had already committed some of his reserves, the Germans had advanced far into some areas of the Soviet defences. During the night 5/6 July, Vatutin transferred the 27th Anti-Tank Brigade to the 6th Guards Army and Chistiakov immediately sent two of its regiments to reinforce the 67th Guards Rifle Division and a third to support the 90th Guards Rifle Division. Although these and other Soviet units raced to the south, the damage to the Voronezh Front had already been done and the Germans prepared to exploit the situation. In addition to sending reinforcements to the 6th Guards Army, Vatutin also transferred formations to the 7th Guards Army sector. Shumilov received control of the 111th and 270th Rifle Divisions from the 69th Army. The 7th Guards Army commander ordered these divisions, along with the 15th Guards Rifle Division, to man the second

Above: Soviet prisoners taken by the SS Leibstandarte *Division rest under guard in the shadow of a building which appears to have been prepared for defence – note the bricks in the window.*

line of defences east of the Koren' River, which was the area in the 24th Guards Rifle Corps' rear. As he assessed the situation, Vatutin realised that, if the enemy's II SS Panzer Corps broke through the 6th Guards Army's defences, it could link up with Army Detachment Kempf. To prevent this occurring, Vatutin deployed the 93rd Guards Rifle Division of the XXXV Guards Rifle Corps to occupy the line east of the Lipovyi-Donetz River and south-west of Prokrovka. By morning, the division had joined the 183rd Rifle Division, while two other XXXV Guards Rifle Corps divisions – the 92nd and the 94th Guards Rifle Divisions – moved up to support the 7th Guards Army. Vatutin expected his troops to defend their positions stubbornly while inflicting heavy damages on the advancing enemy forces.

Throughout the night, both the Soviets and the Germans prepared for a resumption of hostilities on 6 July. Originally, Vatutin had planned to mount a large-scale tank-led counter-attack at dawn, but

General Katukov convinced him to place the tanks of the 1st Tank Army on the defensive instead. Vatutin issued orders to his subordinate officers to dig in and camouflage the tanks. Although the XXXXVIII Panzer Corps and II SS Panzer Corps had made substantial advances on 5 July, Soviet resistance had taken its toll. Hoth planned to attempt a breakout towards Oboian, so he moved up two fresh panzer divisions. Lieutenant General Otto von Knobelsdorff allowed the XXXXVIII Panzer Corps extra time to rest and refit, so it did not resume its offensive until mid-morning on 6 July.

Before any panzer divisions moved out, however, the Germans' artillery fired shells at the Soviet defences for one-and-a-half hours. Following the barrage, the 3rd Panzer, 11th Panzer and *Grossdeutschland* Panzergrenadier Divisions moved against Soviet troops to the north and north-west, forcing them to retreat. German pilots flew 200 sorties of close air support as the advancing panzer divisions drove the 67th Guards Rifle Division back into the 52nd Guards Rifle Division, which was struggling to prevent an enemy breakthrough farther to the east. Because of the Germans' continuous

Right: By 8 July German troops had achieved deep penetrations into the Soviet defences. Soviet commanders transferred reinforcements to the front lines in an attempt to deny the Germans their goal: Prokhorovka.

pressure, Chistiakov finally allowed the two divisions to retreat to positions in and behind the second line of defences. Although the 67th Guards Rifle Division and 52nd Guards Rifle Division withdrew under the weight of the attack, not all of the Germans' efforts were successful. Eight times Knobelsdorff's troops attacked up the Oboian highway against the Soviet second defensive line. Each time, Colonel V. G. Chernov's 90th Guards Rifle Division, with the support of Major General S. M. Krivoshein's III Mechanised Corps, held the line. The fighting intensified as the Germans tried unsuccessfully to breach the line.

By mid-afternoon, the 3rd Panzer Division broke through the last of the enemy defences in the Cherkasskoe sector and advanced to the banks of the Pena River. Soviet defenders fired on the division from the north bank of the river. Upon investigation, the division's commander discovered that the armoured units could not ford the shallow river. As a result, Knobelsdorff shifted the direction of the XXXXVIII Panzer Corps' three-division advance more to the north-east, where the terrain was more suited to tank movement. The 3rd Panzer, 11th Panzer and *Grossdeutschland* Panzergrenadier Divisions moved along the Tomarovka–Oboian road. By late afternoon, forward elements of the *Grossdeutschland* and 11th Panzer Divisions attacked III Mechanised Corps and the 90th Guards Rifle Division, which was dug in along the Lukhanino River. The 35th Anti-Tank Regiment moved forwards to reinforce Krivoshein's III Mechanised Corps. The fighting along the river between Alekseevka and Lukhanino intensified, and the German advance ground to a halt. Despite its initial successes, it had not yet reached its objective, the Psel River; however, the XXXXVIII Panzer Corps was in a good position to renew its offensive on 7 July.

As the Germans advanced east of the Pena River, the threat to the VI Tank Corps lessened. Although he could shift the corps eastwards, Vatutin was concerned about the enemy's II SS Panzer Corps, which

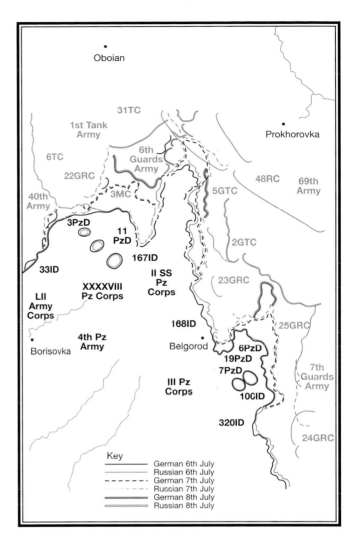

Right: A flamethrower-equipped PzKpfw III tank from the Grossdeutschland *Division clears Soviet defensive lines in front of a fortified village.*

Above: Commander of the Voronezh Front which took the brunt of Army Group South's attack, Nikolai Vatutin. He was killed by Ukrainian nationalists in 1944.

had begun to move towards the centre of the 6th Guards Army's defences. The German panzer corps had already penetrated the defences of the 51st Guards Rifle Division and moved rapidly to the east, despite the V Guards Tank Corps' efforts to stop them. Two panzer divisions forced part of the Soviet division and the 1st Guards Tank Brigade to withdraw to the fortified towns of Prokrovka and Bol'shie Maiachki. Other divisions rapidly advanced another 12km (7$^{1}/_{2}$ miles) and captured two more towns. Although the V Guards Tank Corps counterattacked, the SS panzer divisions shoved them out of the way and shattered the Soviet defences. The 58th Guards Rifle Regiment and elements of the 51st Guards Rifle Infantry Division had no choice but to retreat while the rest of the division and the 1st Guards Tank Brigade desperately clung to Pokrovka and Bol'shie Maiachki. Although the II SS Panzer Corps made great gains on 6 July, Soviet counter-attacks, including one by the II Guard Tank Corps, harassed the corps' flanks. The Soviet harassment gradually became increasingly important.

Late in the day, Vatutin moved more anti-tank units into the battle. The 1st Tank Army Commander,

Katukov, ordered the 100th, 242nd and 237th tank brigades of the XXXI Tank Corps to cut off the German corps' thrust from the west. Krivoshein reinforced Pokrovka with a battalion of the 49th Tank Brigade while the 100th Tank Brigade rushed into Bol'shie Maiachki. As the armoured units arrived, Vatutin withdrew what remained of the 52nd Guards Rifle Division to the rear. For Vatutin, 6 July presented one crisis after another. As the 375th Rifle Division defended a critical area north of Belgorod, part of the 3rd SS Panzergrenadier Division (the *Totenkopf* Division) pushed eastwards towards the Lipovyi-Donetz River. The German division planned to meet Army Detachment Kempf, which was situated east of Belgorod. The 375th Rifle Division's staunch resistance prevented the panzergrenadier division from reaching the river and would have an unforeseen effect on the German's summer offensive.

On 6 July, Army Detachment Kempf confirmed Vatutin's concerns when it burst out of its bridgehead on the Northern Donetz River and threatened the defensive position of the 7th Guards Army. Although the 7th and 19th Panzer Divisions spearheaded the attack, the 6th Panzer Division joined the struggle by late afternoon. The 19th Panzer Division turned to the north-west and hit the left flank and rear of the 81st Guards Rifle Division. Forced out of Belovskoe, a town in the Soviet rear, the 81st Guards Rifle Division quickly deployed its training battalion to stop the German advance. Pushing forwards from the area between Razumnoe and Krutoi Log, the 7th Panzer Division knocked a regiment of the 78th Guards Rifle Division and the 81st Guards Anti-Tank Artillery Battalion out of the way, contained another unit in Krutoi Log and then ran into the Soviet 73rd Guards Rifle Division. The 7th Panzer Division repeatedly hit the defensive positions of the 73rd Guards Rifle Division with frontal assaults throughout the day. Both sides threw themselves into the fierce battle. Colonel S.A. Kozak's 73rd Guards Rifle Division received reinforcement from the 167th and the 262nd Tank regiments and the 1438th Self-propelled Artillery Regiment. Despite repeated attacks by the Germans, the Soviets held the line. Late in the afternoon, however, the 6th Panzer Division reached the front, pushed like a steamroller

Right: Waffen-SS soldiers advance in SdKfz 251 half-tracks. The presence of these hardened fighters in Army Group South's attack undoubtedly contributed to the latter's success against the Soviets.

Above: The Germans did not usually follow the Soviet practice of tank-riding infantry. Here two PzKpfw III tanks create dust as they march past an infantry column. The leading figure carries an anti-tank mine.

over the regiment protecting the Soviet right flank, and occupied a key position between the other two panzer regiments. After Kozak shifted some of his forces to a new line of defence, his troops not only held the line, but also managed to counterattack. As a result, General Kempf had to worry about developing and sustaining Army Detachment Kempf's drive to the north at the same time as Soviet units were threatening his flank.

By the evening of 6 July, however, the 4th Panzer Army had made significant advances. The XXXXVIII Panzer Corps and II SS Panzer Corps had met up near the town of Iakovlevo, which was south of Pokrovka and east of Cherkasskoe, but the losses in armoured vehicles had been high. The Germans, whose campaign was already behind schedule, had to modify their plan. In addition, the Luftwaffe, which had provided air support for the two panzer corps, had lost more than 100 aircraft. The aircraft losses and the diminishing supply of aviation fuel meant that the Luftwaffe's ability to support the ground troops became increasingly limited. On 6 July, while German pilots flew 873 sorties over the battlefield, their Soviet counterparts flew 1278.

The Voronezh Front commander also faced a number of problems, including a large hole in his front. Although the Germans had not yet achieved their objectives, they had inflicted severe damage upon the Soviet main line of resistance. The 7th Guards Army alone had repelled 12 German attacks on 6 July. In addition, with the exception of three of the 69th Army's divisions, Vatutin had already committed all of his front reserves. In some areas, the defences were not up to full strength. Soviet troops manned two or three defensive lines along the Prokhorovka and Korocha axes; however, they only occupied the army second line along the Oboian axis. When Vatutin informed Stalin of the situation on the Voronezh Front, he transferred the 27th Army from Steppe Front to the southern part of the salient. Although he agreed to the commander's request for more reinforcements, Stalin reiterated his standing orders: Soviet forces were to fight battles of attrition and to hold the Germans along the prepared defences until it was time to begin the offensive operations in all areas of the front. Marshal Alexander Vasilevsky, after consultation with Marshal Georgi Zhukov, suggested that Stalin approve the deployment of the previously uncommitted II Tank Corps and X Tank Corps to the Prokhorovka area. Despite the objections of the Steppe Front commander, Army General Ivan Konev, Stavka assumed control of the 5th Guards Tank Army and ordered it to move to Staryi Oskol, north-east of Prokhorovka.

Early on 7 July, Vatutin initiated steps to allow his front to hold on for a couple of days until the powerful reinforcements arrived. Wanting to take advantage of the previous day's successes, the II SS Panzer Corps and XXXXVIII Panzer Corps renewed their attacks against the 6th Guards Army and the 1st Tank Army, which had been reinforced with Vatutin's remaining armoured and anti-tank units. The German attack pre-empted any assault planned by Vatutin and created a crisis. While more than 300 tanks, supported by motorised infantry and air attacks, assaulted Soviet positions around Pokrovka, another 100 tanks moved against Bol'shie Maiachki. At the same time, other German formations hit the rear of the 6th Guards and 1st Tank Armies. The weight of the enemy assault forced the 49th and 100th tank brigades to withdraw from key defensive positions by the end of the day. Katukov called for air support and Soviet dive-bombers arrived to strafe the attacking enemy. The Germans broke through the centre of 51st Guards Rifle Division's defences. As II SS Panzer Corps formations moved up the Prokhorovka road, they drove back the Soviets' V Guards Tank Corps; however, the German corps' flanks became extended and vulnerable. Chernienko's XXXI Tank Corps moved towards the II SS Panzer Corps' left flank. As Knobelsdorff shifted units around to protect his flanks, he also concentrated his forward units in a determined effort to destroy the Soviet armoured formations in his way.

Even more serious than the SS panzer corps' advance was the threat to Krivoshein's III Mechanised Corps. Only four brigades defended the river area between Alekseevka and Pokrovka. Krivoshein had few reinforcements for his front line of 200 dug-in tanks. The 1st Guards Tank Brigade, the corps' premier unit, was already locked in a fierce battle with II SS Panzer Corps forces near Pokrovka. Vatutin frantically tried to find additional forces to send in support of the III Mechanised Corps. Early on 7 July, the XXXXVIII Panzer Corps attacked and cut through Krivoshein's defences. The 1st Tank Army's defensive front was in danger of breaking and the German corps threatened the XXXI Soviet Tank Corps' flank. Supported by 40 Panthers and waves of dive-bombers, the German tanks slowly pushed their way through the Soviet defences and forced the defenders to retreat. As Krivoshein's

forces gave way, the XI Tank Corps moved east to support the III Mechanised Corps by attacking the Germans' flank.

As the XXXXVIII Panzer Corps' thrust continued on 8 July, it moved up the Oboian road and pushed against what remained of the III Mechanised Corps. During the intense fighting, a German breakthrough seemed imminent. Vatutin ordered a withdrawal of Chernienko's XXXI Tank Corps and the remnants of III Mechanised Corps to a new defensive line across the Oboian road north of Verkhopen'e. He sent a rifle division, an anti-tank brigade, two tank brigades and three anti-tank regiments to meet them. The new position was tied to VI Tank Corps' defences. Vatutin hoped that the two reinforced corps could hold their position until the counter-attacks by the II Tank, X Tank and V Guards Tank corps south of Prokhorovka had an effect. Darkness and heavy

Below: An SS soldier stands guard over a Soviet prisoner attending to his wounded comrade. In the background is a T-34 which has literally been blown apart by a large explosion.

Above: German tanks – either PzKpfw III or IVs – wait for the order to attack again. The reserves of tanks carefully gathered by Guderian over the winter were fast disappearing as a result of the offensive.

Below: Waffen-SS troops race from their Schwimmwagen to set up an MG 42 machine gun on the outskirts of Gostishchevo. The loader carries two boxes of ammunition containing 250 round belts.

Soviet artillery fire finally halted the movement of the forward divisions of the XXXXVIII Panzer Corps.

The end appeared to be in sight. Knobelsdorff believed that the XXXXVIII Panzer Corps could tear through the enemy's defences along the Oboian road, cross the Psel River and reach Kursk. The VI Soviet Tank Corps' threat to his left flank, however, posed a problem. In addition, intelligence reports suggested an enemy infantry build-up in the region. Knobelsdorff ordered the *Grossdeutschland* and 11th Panzer Divisions to move forwards and be prepared to capture the high ground at Hill 260.8 early on 9 July. They were then to join the 3rd Panzer and 332nd Infantry Divisions' westward assault to destroy the Soviet armoured force near Verkhopen'e. Once these divisions eliminated the threat to XXXXVIII Panzer Corps' flank, they would resume the advance on Oboian and Kursk.

Knobelsdorff expected the II SS Panzer Corps to renew its attack from Prokhorovka to Kursk at the same time. On 8 July, II SS Panzer Corps had turned in a more northerly direction. Once the II SS Panzer Corps straightened its line, two panzergrenadier regiments began to push back one of XXXI Tank Corps' tank brigades. As it covered its right flank, the German panzer corps moved slowly towards the Psel River. Vatutin planned to launch an attack before the enemy could regroup and resume the offensive. Failure to be totally prepared before the counter-attack began, however, meant that elements of the 183rd Rifle Division entered the battle in a piecemeal fashion. German anti-tank fire mauled the division. The II Soviet Tank Corps arrived on the scene late. Its commander, General Markian Popov, did not concentrate the corps for a unified attack. Hence it suffered the same fate as the 183rd Rifle Division. Kravchenko's V Guards Tank Corps made little headway in its attack against an entrenched *Deutschland* Regiment. German aircraft, along with a panzergrenadier regiment, thrashed the II Guards Tank Corps, which lost no less than 50 tanks when its assault was repulsed. The fire from the 30mm (1.18in) automatic cannon of four squadrons of Henschel Hs129 aircraft played a large role in disrupting the Soviet tank attack. The II SS Panzer Corps appeared to be unstoppable.

German advances in the 7th Guards Army area were not, however, as dramatic as they were on the 4th Panzer Army's front. The intense battle that continued around Belgorod hindered Army Detachment Kempf's movements. As the 7th Guards Army continued to receive reinforcements, German efforts to penetrate its defences failed. On 7 July, the III Panzer Corps planned to turn northwards and outflank the enemy's 81st Guards Rifle Division. The Soviet defenders refused to give ground, and went on to counterattack Army Detachment Kempf's right flank. By late afternoon, forward units of the 6th and 7th Panzer Divisions and two divisions of the XXXV Guards Rifle Corps clashed east of Belgorod, as the Soviet rifle corps moved up to reinforce the XXV Guards Rifle Corps. Although the 19th Panzer Division met with initial successes, it failed to penetrate the Soviet defences and destroy the salient that had formed around Belgorod. To meet the III Panzer

Below: Hermann Hoth, commander of the 4th Panzer Army. Hoth had led tank formations in Poland, France and the Soviet Union, but he was removed from his command by Hitler in November 1943.

Corps threat on 7 July, Shumilov ordered the 92nd Guards Rifle Division and 94th Guards Rifle Division into the line and deployed tank and anti-tank units to support them. The next day, however, the 6th Panzer Division broke through the defences, and Colonel A. F. Vasilev's reserve 305th Rifle Division received orders to create a new line of defence to block the 6th Panzer Division's advance.

The German forces punched a hole in the Voronezh Front's main line of resistance on the first day of the campaign against the southern face of the Kursk salient and continued to push north towards their primary objective, Kursk. During the next three days of the campaign – 6–8 July – the 4th Panzer Army and Army Detachment Kempf penetrated the Soviets' first and second lines of defence, and the battle raged in the 10km (6 mile) zone between the second and third defensive lines. Although their progress improved on 8 July, the two German armies had only advanced 20km ($12^{1}/_{2}$ miles) from their starting point. Kursk was still 100km (60 miles) away.

Despite their extensive defences, the Soviets failed to prevent the German penetration of their main line of resistance. The weight of the tank attack proved

Above: Battle-weary German soldiers take a break before going into action against Soviet positions around Podolyan. The man on the left has an MG 34 machine gun and a stick grenade in his belt.

overwhelming in places. That did not mean, however, that the Soviets would give up the fight or retreat beyond their next line of defences. From the beginning, the critical nature of the situation persuaded Vatutin to commit many of his reserves during the first few days of the campaign. Numerous Soviet formations, including seven armoured corps, counterattacked the advancing enemy repeatedly from all sides. They slowed the German advance as much as possible as more reinforcements rushed to Vatutin's

Below: An SS squad prepares to join the battle on 8 July 1943 which the smoky haze obscures from view. On the right, a mortar detachment carrying their weapon and ammunition await their orders.

Voronezh Front. The Soviets were determined to make the enemy's progress costly. It was true that the Germans had broken through the first two defensive lines, but six more blocked their path to Kursk. According to their plan, the Germans had to close the salient in six days if they hoped to destroy the Soviet forces within it. The cessation of hostilities on 8 July signalled the end of the fourth day. Instead of advancing an average of 20km ($12^1/_2$ miles) a day, the total movement after four days was 20km ($12^1/_2$ miles). The number of reserve units arriving in the Voronezh Front area greatly increased by the night of 8 July. The Germans were rapidly becoming outnumbered. Field Marshal Erich von Manstein, the Army Group South (AGS) commander, had no idea of the extent of the reserves upon which the Stavka could draw. The field marshal believed that a major breakthrough on 9 July was still possible. Once the Germans had completely broken through the Soviet defences, their rate of advance towards Kursk would increase dramatically.

As the fighting ended on 8 July, Soviet and German commanders seriously assessed the situation and contemplated their actions for the next day. The crucial decisions made on the night 8/9 July would

Above: Waffen-SS soldiers, complete with a signals section, take advantage of a pause in the fighting to rest and recuperate from the gruelling struggle they face against the determined Soviet resistance.

determine the battle of Kursk's outcome. The most serious challenges confronting Vatutin, Stavka's representative Marshal Alexander Vasilevsky, and the Soviet General Staff itself, were those of strengthening the defences in the Voronezh Front area and preparing for the planned counter-attack. Before the counter-offensive could begin, however, Soviet forces had to stop the German advance, while at the same time causing massive casualties. This meant that the defence of the Oboian–Kursk axis had to be successful. As they pondered the problem, the Soviet commanders identified two solutions: the construction of impenetrable defences along the road leading to Oboian and the continuation of counter-attacks against both the Germans' forward attacking elements and the panzer corps' flanks. Both of these options were a continuation of what they had been doing since the beginning. Two factors made this decision easier. First, the Western Front and Briansk Front forces had assisted the Central Front troops in stopping the 9th German Army's offensive; these forces would soon mount their own attack north and east of Orel. Secondly, the powerful Steppe Front forces, commanded by General I. S. Konev, had moved up and could, when necessary, have decisive impact on the battle. The Stavka proceeded to issue a series of new orders on 9 July.

Following the recommendation of Vasilevsky and Vatutin to hasten the build-up of strategic reserves, Stavka transferred the 5th Guards Tank Army from Steppe Front to Voronezh Front. Commanded by Lieutenant General P. A. Rotmistrov, the 5th Guards Tank Army travelled more than 200km (125 miles) from the region west of the Don River to the Staryi Oskol region, where it arrived on 8 July. Rotmistrov received orders from Stavka to move his army to the Prokhorovka region quickly. To limit the army's vulnerability to enemy air attack, it moved only at night and had almost reached its new assembly area by

Below: Three Waffen-SS soldiers at Kursk. The squatting figure is armed with a Soviet PPSh 41 submachine gun, which was favoured by both sides for its reliability and large magazine.

2300 hours on 9 July. The 5th Guards Tank Army had 593 tanks and 37 self-propelled guns, as well as thousands of artillery pieces, motor transports and support vehicles. Rotmistrov had orders to deploy his forward elements to the line of the Psel River and areas west of Prokhorovka by 10 July.

Vatutin and Vasilevsky made other recommendations with which the Supreme High Command concurred. Stavka also informed Lieutenant General A. S. Zhadov that control of his 5th Guards Army would shift from Steppe Front to Voronezh Front. Zhadov received instructions to move the army's two guards rifle corps – the XXXII Guards Rifle Corps and the XXXIII Guards Rifle Corps – into the region along the Psel River between Oboian and Prokhorovka. It would take several days for the 80,000-strong army to fulfill the Stavka order. In addition, Stavka assigned the responsibility for defending the Prokhorovka–Lipovyi Donetz River sector, which lay between the 6th and 7th Guards Armies, to the 69th Army. Lieutenant General V. D. Kriuchenkin, the commander of the 69th Army, immediately got to work. He moved up the 93rd Guards Rifle Division of the XXXV Guards Rifle Corps to bolster the Lipovyi–Donetz line. Kriuchenkin made preparations for the defence of the crucial river sector with the 183rd, 89th Guards and 81st Guards Rifle Divisions. The 69th Army commander then deployed the 92nd Guards, 94th Guards and 305th Rifle Divisions east of the Northern Donetz River, where they could challenge the III German Panzer Corps' advance.

While Stavka issued transfer orders to various commands, Vatutin strengthened the defences within the Voronezh Front, particularly along the Oboian road, by conducting a general regrouping of his forces. Vatutin began to regroup his forces in the early morning hours of 9 July. General Burkov received orders to transfer his X Tank Corps defences along the Prokhorovka road to General Popov's command. Popov's II Tank Corps would occupy the defences and the X Tank Corps became attached to Katukov's 1st Tank Army. Vatutin ordered Burkov to deploy the tank corps westwards. Its job was to delay the II SS Panzer Corps' advance towards Kochetovka, where Soviet troops had constructed new lines of defence. After slowing the Germans, the X Tank Corps would take up a new defensive position at Vladimirovka along the Oboian road. Ordered to join Katukov's defence by 10 July, Kravchenko prepared to move his V Guards Tank

Corps from south of Prokhorovka. Once they were in position, the X Tank Corps and V Guards Tank Corps could support the 1st Tank Army's defensive efforts or attack the left flank of the XXXXVIII Panzer Corps, which rested alongside the Pena River. Vatutin deployed other formations, including tank, anti-tank and artillery regiments, to bolster Katukov's 1st Tank Army.

Vatutin expected the 1st Tank, 6th Guards and 69th Armies to maintain their defensive positions and prohibit a German advance to Oboian and Prokhorovka. The Soviet Army commanders carried out their preparations in the early morning hours of 9 July. General Hoth, the commander of the 4th Panzer Army, used the night 8/9 July to concentrate his forces for a renewal of the movement towards Oboian and Kursk. Hoth had his sights set on Kursk and believed that the forward elements of the XXXXVIII Panzer and II SS Panzer Corps could reach the town. Field Marshal von Manstein ordered all available aircraft to provide maximum air support for the advancing ground forces. During the day, German aircraft would fly more than 1500 sorties over the battlefield and the Soviet defences. The Germans would aim their primary thrusts against the Belgorod–Oboian highway sector. One of XXXXVIII Panzer Corps' principal concerns was the threat to its left flank. Knobelsdorff ordered the *Grossdeutschland*, 3rd Panzer and 332nd Infantry Divisions to

Right: A German assault gun battalion supporting a reconnaissance unit advancing on the town of Verkopenye. The wide open plains allowed tanks to engage each other at long distances.

Above: While wide-open spaces facilitated the transfer of tanks to the front, as shown here by the T-34s in this photograph, they also left the tanks exteremely vulnerable to enemy attacks from the air.

eliminate the flank threat, while the 11th Panzer Division, along with some elements of the *Grossdeutschland* Division, met up with the II SS Panzer Corps to continue the move towards Oboian and Kursk. Hoth ordered the II SS Panzer Corps to advance towards Kursk on 9 July. The *Das Reich* and the 167th Infantry Divisions would provide flank support. The majority of II SS Panzer Corps' 283 tanks and artillery guns would lead the drive to Kursk.

Initially, the German advance went as planned. Two of the II SS Panzer Corps' panzergrenadier divisions – the *Leibstandarte* and *Totenkopf* – pushed through the III Mechanised Corps, which had already been mauled by the Germans. These units

Above: The SU-152 made its combat debut at Kursk, where it destroyed 12 Tigers and 7 Ferdinands. Here German soldiers examine an example stuck in mud that has been abandoned by its crew.

then forced the XXXI Tank Corps to retreat north-wards back to Kochetovka. By the end of the day, the *Totenkopf* Panzergrenadier Division arrived at the Psel River and, after a short but fierce battle, seized the village of Krasnyi Oktiabr from the remaining elements of the 52nd Guards Rifle Division and X Tank Corps Motorised Rifle Brigade. The *Leibstandarte* Panzergrenadier Division crossed the Solotinka River, captured a village and met up with the 11th Panzer Division.

In the meantime, the X Soviet Tank Corps regrouped in time to stop the *Leibstandarte* and 11th Panzer Divisions outside Kochetovka. Elements of the II SS Panzer Corps continued their advance towards Prokhorovka. The II Tank Corps and V Guards Corps repeatedly attacked the German divi-sion in an effort to prevent it from reaching Prokhorovka. Late in the afternoon, the Soviet

attacks became less frequent as the V Guards Corps withdrew to take up its next position.

As the II SS Panzer Corps continued towards Prokhorovka, the XXXXVIII Panzer Corps resumed its attack. On the morning of 9 July, the full force of the XXXXVIII Panzer Corps' armour showed its might and pushed northwards towards the town of Novoselovkaon. However, by the end of the day, the strong resistance from the Soviets had prevented the Germans from advancing any farther than the out-skirts of the town. In addition, the Soviets impaired their performance by forcing the corps to split and move in two separate directions. The 11th Panzer Division, which moved up the Oboian road, broke through the defences of the III Mechanised Corps and captured Hill 260.8, south of Novoselovkaon. After linking up with the *Leibstandarte* Panzergrenadier Division, it continued its march to the north. However, despite making this progress, by the end of the day the 309th Soviet Rifle Division, which was supported by strong anti-tank and artillery fire, forced the 11th Panzer Division to stop south of its objective. Yet further south, Army Detachment Kempf's III Panzer Corps made very little progress against the Soviet defences. In addition, Army Detachment Kempf had failed to prevent the enemy's 5th Guards Tank Army from linking up with the 1st Tank Army.

Throughout the day, German aircraft provided the ground troops with much-needed support, primarily along the Oboian–Kursk axis. German pilots flew twice as many sorties as the Soviets, but for all of their efforts, it was not enough, and the 4th Panzer Army failed to reach the main objectives it had been set for that day.

The Germans' last major attempt at a frontal assault took place on 9 July, and was intended to break through the Soviet defences and advance to the region around Oboian. From this point, it was believed, they would be able to launch an offensive against Kursk. It did not succeed. By the end of the day, despite the armoured thrusts and the intense fighting, the Germans had only managed to force the Soviets to retreat the short distance of 6–8km ($3\frac{3}{4}$ to 5 miles) to the north.

The cost to the Germans was high. The Soviets destroyed almost 300 German tanks and a large number of self-propelled guns, armoured transports and motor vehicles during the fighting on that day.

Late in the afternoon, as Vatutin consolidated his forces and moved up reinforcements in preparation for the next day, Hoth made a decision that had important consequences.

Based on the day's limited progress and the loss of tanks and other equipment, he decided to alter his offensive plans. He ordered the II SS Panzer Corps to turn to the north-east and march towards Prokhorovka. The commander of the 4th Panzer Army also asked the Luftwaffe to attack in a more easterly direction. Hoth counted on the combination of a powerful panzer corps and intense air support. This force, he thought, would be able to crush the armoured threat in the east, break through the Soviet defences, and open a new route to Kursk. If the 9th Army could then penetrate southwards, the two armies could band together and achieve Operation Citadel's objective.

Hoth would discover, however, that the change in his plans would result in a totally different outcome than the one he had imagined, and his forces would soon be engaged in a historic tank battle of totally unprecedented proportions.

Below: A barefoot German gunner rests near his light anti-tank gun. He has dug a slit trench visible in the foreground for protection against enemy artillery or air attack.

CHAPTER SEVEN

Last Efforts in the North

The Balance Shifts

Repeated attacks had brought the Germans very little territory at the cost of high casualties. Model reluctantly agreed to another attack, but the Soviet commanders decided the time had come to go on the offensive themselves.

During the first five days of the Battle for Kursk, the 9th German Army and the Soviets' 13th Army and 2nd Tank Army clashed along the northern part of the Kursk bulge. The horrific fighting caused heavy casualties in men and materiel on both sides. Attacking from the area around Orel, the Germans expected to pierce the Soviet's Central Front defences north of Kursk quickly. According to the German plan, the 9th Army would reach Kursk within two to three days. By 9 July, not only had the Germans not made major advances into the Soviet front, but they also faced a crisis.

The previous day, the first of many crises unfolded. Forward elements of the XXXXVII Panzer Corps attempted to break away from General Konstantin Rokossovsky's tank reserves. Once free from the Soviet tanks, it would be able to advance rapidly across the open terrain to Kursk. Instead, the panzer corps stumbled into a heavily fortified ridge located south-west of Ol'khovatka. Bad weather prevented the Luftwaffe from providing vital air support. The XXXXVII Panzer Corps' advance halted for the day. The brutal fighting caused more casualties and resulted in only minimal gains. As the panzer corps

Left: Model's 9th Army could not match 4th Panzer Army's level of success in the south. Never a strong advocate of Citadel, Model knew his forces could not keep sustaining such losses against Soviet troops like those shown here.

Above: PzKpfw IIIs and IVs of 9th Army prepare for another push against the Soviet lines. However the Red Army would soon force Model onto the defensive.

regrouped during the night, General Walter Model reluctantly gave the order to attack the ridge the next day. The XXXXVII Panzer Corps resumed the assault on 9 July. An air and artillery barrage preceded the renewed attack, but it failed to lessen Soviet resistance. The fighting along the Ol'khovatka–Ponyri road intensified and the Germans advanced slowly. Ferocious fighting continued along the front, but particularly in the areas near the villages of Teploe, Ol'khovatka and Ponyri. Each time the German infantry-supported tanks attacked and gained a small amount of territory, a Soviet counter-thrust by armour, artillery and rifle formations forced them back. Control of Teploe and parts of Ponyri switched back and forth between the Germans and the Soviets. As the advantage see-sawed from one side to the other, the losses mounted. In the end, however, as the day's struggle ceased, the Soviets frequently held the field in any fought-for territory. The 2nd Tank Army played a key role in the battle as the Soviets fiercely resisted the enemy's repeated efforts to advance.

As the Germans' progress declined, that of their enemy improved. The Soviets launched counter-attacks, forcing the enemy corps – the 13th Army and the XXXXI, XXXXVI and XXXXVII Panzer Corps – to switch from offensive to defensive tactics. Consequently, the 9th Army made little progress on 9 July and the possibility of the situation improving on 10 July was slim. Casualties were mounting: approximately 50,000 troops lost and 400 tanks and assault guns, as well as 500 aircraft, destroyed. German losses outnumbered replacements. As he assessed the situation, the commander of the 9th Army reached certain conclusions. The Citadel plan demanded a quick breakthrough. Thus far, it had not happened. The 9th Army had not yet achieved the goals set for the first day. No matter how he examined it, Model could see that, even if his forces captured the ridge, they could not break through to Kursk quickly. In addition, the 9th Army's forces were exhausted; this factor had persuaded Model to rest his forces during the afternoon of 9 July. Based upon the losses already suffered by the 9th Army, Model also concluded that, as the campaign continued, in all likelihood it would be an attritional battle. The fact that the Soviet forces still appeared strong did not help. Never a staunch supporter of the Citadel offensive, the German general became increasingly distressed about the 9th Army's chances as the days passed. Although the idea of an attritional offensive was a disturbing one, Model gave his orders to prepare for the next day.

The Soviets also prepared themselves. Model may not have been confident that the 9th Army could take the ridge and continue on to Kursk, but General

Rokossovsky's confidence that the troops manning the Central Front defences could stop the enemy advance still grew. Prior to the start of the battle, the Soviets had attempted to construct a defensive system that the enemy's tanks could not penetrate. They had constructed a series of anti-tank lines and filled the strong points with artillery. Stavka chose to concentrate the main Soviet artillery forces in the 13th Army and 70th Army sectors. The 13th Army's defences contained 13 anti-tank areas with 44 strongly fortified positions in the main line of resistance (MLR). The second line had 9 areas with 34 strongholds, while the third line had 15 anti-tank positions with 60 strengthened areas. On the first day, the Germans had breached the main line of resistance in places, but they had not penetrated the second line. Thus far under enemy attack, the Soviet network of defences had bent, but not broken. Rokossovsky brought more reserves to the front. He ordered the defences strengthened and his forces consolidated in the most-threatened areas. As had been the case over the past few days, however, Rokossovsky also issued attack orders. According to the Soviet plan, whenever possible, each German thrust would be followed by a counter-attack.

Despite the situation on the 9th Army's front, the Führer remained committed to the campaign. Because Hitler refused to authorise retreat and because of the exhausted state of his army, Model set modest objectives for 10 July. He assigned a strictly defensive role to the XXIII Army Corps and XXXXI Panzer Corps. The XXXXVI and XXXXVII Panzer Corps would renew the attack against the Soviet defences near Teploe and against the flank of the 70th Army. As the XXXXVII Panzer Corps owned most of the 9th Army's tanks, Model ordered it to proceed southwards 5km (3 miles) and to take the high ground near Molotychi. By this time, Panzer Brigade Burmeister included three panzer divisions: the 2nd, 4th and 20th. General Joachim Lemelsen, the commander of XXXXVII Panzer Corps, received orders to place Panzer Brigade Burmeister near Samodurovka, which was north of Teploe, as part of the 9th Army Reserve. Model would call upon Panzer Brigade Burmeister as he needed reserve forces. He received a promise from the Luftwaffe for all-out air support of the attack by XXXXVII Panzer Corps on 10 July. Despite the dismal hope for a success, the XXXXVI Panzer Corps and XXXXVII Panzer Corps prepared to return to the offensive.

On 10 July, the battle in the north continued in full force. With the support of elements of the 2nd, 4th and 20th Panzer Divisions, Lemelsen's XXXXVII Panzer Corps began its thrust towards Teploe. Intense fighting erupted in the difficult terrain north of the village. The Soviets fired heavy artillery and mortar shells at the advancing enemy. Soviet aircraft strafed and bombed the XXXXVII Panzer Corps' forward units as they tried to inch their way towards Teploe. Burning tanks began to litter the field. The panzer corps· continued to hit the Soviet defences, but the defenders stood firm. Within a couple of hours, the German advance stalled. Soviet artillery and mortar shells fell incessantly on the stonewalled enemy. Lemelsen reluctantly reported the situation to Model, who decided to call off the attack. By

Below: PzKpfw IV tanks move through a blasted landscape. In summer 1943, elderly tanks like the PzKpfw IIIs and IVs still formed much of the German panzer arm, particularly in the northern sector.

noon on 10 July, Model ordered the XXXXVII Panzer Corps formations to stop their forward movement and to retreat to their original positions.

The Soviets quickly took advantage of the situation. Rokossovsky ordered an attack to be made. General N. P. Pukhov, commander of the 13th Army, and General Aleksei Rodin, the 2nd Tank Army commander, quickly made preparations. By the afternoon, they were ready. The 1st Guards Artillery Division provided support and the attack by elements of the 2nd Tank Army and the XIX Tank Corps began. Three rifle divisions – the 40th, the 70th Guards and the 75th Guards Rifle Divisions – followed the tanks as they pursued the Germans back to their defensive positions.

While the XXXXVII Panzer Corps tangled with the Soviet tanks and rifle divisions, the XXXXVI Panzer Corps prepared to implement its orders. On the night 9/10 July, Model had ordered General Zorn to make preparations to attack the east flank of the Soviet 70th Army. Commanded by General I. V. Galanin,

the 70th Army defended the region west of the 2nd Tank Army. Protecting the area between the two Soviet armies were the XIX Tank Corps and XVI Tank Corps. Six rifle divisions – the 106th, the 211th, the 280th, the 132nd, the 175th and the 140th – manned the front lines of the 70th Army's sector with the support of tank and artillery units. Zorn chose the 258th, the 7th, and the 31st Infantry Divisions to lead the assault. The 258th German Infantry Division took the lead and launched an assault against the 280th Soviet Rifle Division. The Soviet rifle division stood firm and gave up little ground, and mounted two counter-attacks against the German infantry division. The 258th Infantry Division managed to capture a hill, but a counter-attack by the Soviet rifle division forced it to retreat. The 7th German Infantry Division attempted to penetrate the defences of the 175th Soviet Rifle Division, but a Soviet counter-attack with T-34s compelled it to withdraw.

As a result of the failure of the 258th Infantry Division's and 7th Infantry Division's attacks, the XXXXVI Panzer Corps failed to make any progress. By the end of the day, the position of both panzer corps was the same as it had been when they attacked in the morning.

Below: Soviet snipers lie in wait in a camouflaged trench for the enemy to attack. The Red Army set great score by snipers, often former Siberian hunters used to handling a rifle.

On 10 July, the fierce struggle for control of Ponyri continued. Late the night before, Model issued orders to the commander of XXXXI Panzer Corps to maintain a defensive position the next day. Although the panzer corps did not go on the offensive, it experienced heavy fighting on 10 July. The III Soviet Tank Corps moved up to assist the 307th Rifle Division in its defence of the town against the enemy's 292nd Infantry Division. During the morning, a Soviet assault commenced with an artillery and air bombardment. The 5th Artillery Division opened fire as Soviet aircraft strafed and bombed the positions held by the 86th Infantry Division and the 10th Panzer Grenadier Division. Model had recently deployed the 10th Panzergrenadier Division, which had originally been part of his reserves, to the XXXXI Panzer Corps sector. After the artillery and air attack, the Soviet tanks assaulted the German positions near Ponyri in the 307th Rifle Division's area. The Soviets did not, however, follow the tank assault with strong infantry attacks. By late afternoon, approximately six Soviet tanks took a hill near Ponyri, but their victory was short-lived. Soon afterwards, German Stukas arrived on the scene. They attacked the Soviet tanks

Above: A German machine gun team move out of a position that has largely been destroyed by fighting. Both men carry entrenching tools to allow them to dig a slit trench for cover.

and forced them to withdraw. Control of Ponyri changed hands several times. The German assault on the area west of the railroad at the junction between the 13th and 70th Armies continued. As the fighting spread, the Germans succeeded in seizing Teploe, but the Soviet defenders prevented them from advancing further. Although the Germans forced them to withdraw from Teploe, the Soviets still controlled the high ground in the region. The Soviets continued to occupy the commanding heights between Kutyrki and Molotychi.

Not all of the Soviet activity of 10 July was defensive in nature. In addition to stopping the German thrusts and counter attacking, the Soviets initiated their own offensive operations. The situation heated up on the front between the XV Soviet Corps and the XXIII German Corps. Early in the morning on 10 July, forward units of two Soviet rifle divisions – the 74th and 148th – assaulted the Germans at Protasovo, a village slightly north and west of

Above: As had been the case in earlier battles, the Soviets did not plan to remain on the defensive. After allowing the Germans to attack and suffer losses, Soviet troops launched a counter-attack.

Maloarkhangel'sk. Situated at Protasovo, the 78th Sturm Infantry Division XXIII Corps bore the brunt of the Soviet attack, which had strong tank and air support. Although they lost a dozen tanks, the Soviet troops gained some ground against the Germans. The fighting near Protasovo intensified, as the Soviet 12th Artillery Division repeatedly fired shells at the German 78th Sturm Infantry Division. The Soviet artillery division also shelled the enemy's 216th Infantry Division. Despite the artillery attack, the 78th Sturm Infantry Division not only held on, but also gained some ground. General Johannes Freissner, the commander of the XXIII Corps, ordered some Ferdinands to the front. With the support of the Ferdinands, part of the 78th Sturm Infantry Division captured a hill near Trossna. By the early afternoon, the German division captured the town of Trossna and took over 800 Soviet prisoners.

The day ended with heavy losses in men and materiel by both sides. The brutal attacks and counter-attacks bore little result. Both German panzer corps – the XXXXVI Panzer Corps and the XXXXVII Panzer Corps – failed to advance. Any ground that

they took early in the day, the Soviets forced them to relinquish by day's end. The Soviet attacks were equally unsuccessful. Not only did the Soviet attacks fail to force the Germans to withdraw, but also the attack against the XXIII German Corps resulted in the Soviet's loss of Trossna. As the fighting ended on 10 July, both the Germans and the Soviets once again evaluated the situation.

As Model reviewed the day's events, he realised that not much had changed since the day before. The 9th Army had again failed to force its way through the strong anti-tank defences of the 13th Army. The entrenched tanks of the 2nd Tank Army and the XIX Tank Corps had provided the Soviets with a strong, virtually impenetrable defensive network. With the exception of the first day of the campaign, the frontal assaults against the enemy's defences had not worked. Model had little option, however, but to launch frontal attacks. A continuation of strong attacks would require enormous reserves in men, tanks, munitions and other materials. Model did not have access to a limitless supply of these kinds of reserves. In fact, the first six days of the offensive had steadily drained Model's reserves and he had not received enough reinforcements of men or replacement equipment. Hitler had denied Model's most recent request for replacement troops.

Right: A mortar crew duck for cover as they fire another round towards the enemy, while another soldier watches from a distance. A good mortar crew could have several shells in the air at the same time.

Furthermore, the situation on other Germans fronts had changed, which made the possibility of Model receiving more reinforcements even less likely.

While Model planned and executed yet another attack against the Soviet defences, Hitler faced another crisis. The Führer notified Model of recent events in the Mediterranean. During the night 9/10 July, an Allied armada carrying invasion troops sailed from North Africa to Sicily. Only two German divisions protected the island: the Germans relied upon Italian troops to help defend it. Allied air superiority prevented adequate support for the Axis ground troops by the Luftwaffe. Reports about the situation on Sicily suggested that the Italian troops were now discarding their weapons and fleeing. Although the situation on the Eastern Front had also reached crisis proportions, Hitler decided that it was more important to meet the new threat in the Mediterranean. Therefore, he ordered reinforcements sent to Kesselring in Italy, not to Model in the Soviet Union. Although the situation in the Mediterranean would later cause him to reconsider a

continuation of Operation Citadel, on the night 10/11 July, Hitler would not allow Model to order a retreat. He had to continue to press the offensive.

As much as he personally might have wanted to end the campaign, quitting was not an option. Therefore, during the night 10/11 July, Model decided to turn to his reserves once again. The 292nd Infantry Division had been particularly hard

Below: One Soviet soldier remains on watch for an attack while a female medical attendant helps his wounded comrade. Note the blanket rolls which were also used to carry food and supplies inside.

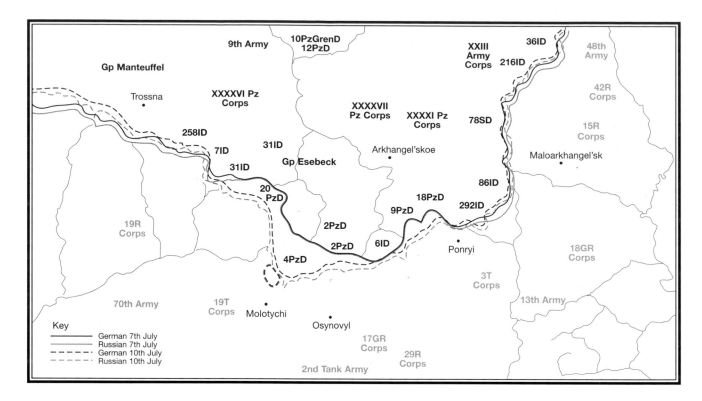

Above: The German 9th Army's advance into the Central Front's defences between 7 July and 10 July were extremely limited and, for some days afterwards, they suffered ferocious Soviet counter-attacks.

hit in the fighting around Ponyri, so Model pulled it out of the line and ordered the 10th Panzergrenadier Division to take its place. Commanded by Lieutenant General August Schmidt, the 10th Panzergrenadier Division had an especially strong artillery unit. The division contained seven artillery battalions, a Nebelwerfer regiment, a heavy mortar battalion and an assault-gun battalion. A Nebelwerfer was a rocket launcher that had multiple launch rails and fired 300mm (11.9in) high-explosive rockets. When fired, red streaks pierce the smoke as the rocket projectiles flew off the rails and through the sky towards their targets. The blast and ear-splitting noise from a Nebelwerfer could unnerve even the most battle-hardened soldiers.

Before he completed his plans for the next day, Model met with Lemelsen, the commander of XXXXVII Panzer Corps. Both commanders were aware that the Soviets had begun to deploy fresh troops along the front across from the panzer corps' positions. However, After six days of intense fighting, the men of the panzer corps were exhausted; they were battle weary. Model and Lemelsen agreed that an attack on 11 July by XXXXVII Panzer Corps

was not possible. In fact, it could be disastrous. Consequently, Model decided that the corps would only provide supporting fire. Model explained his decision to the Army Group Centre (AGC) commander, Field Marshal Günther von Kluge. Kluge finally accepted the reality of the situation and agreed to the deployment of the 12th Panzer Division from Model's reserves to the XXXXVII Panzer Corps. Because he thought it prudent to provide even more reinforcements for the corps, Kluge made plans to transfer the 5th and 8th Panzer Divisions from the AGC reserves to the Kursk front.

On 11 July, the Soviets pounded the panzer divisions with a vengeance. Although the fighting since 5 July had been intense, the fierceness of the Soviet assault surprised the Germans. Not all of the 10th Panzergrenadier Division formations had yet reached the front lines, but the artillery units that had arrived were powerful enough to repel a series of enemy counter-attacks. As the rest of the artillery units moved to the front, they joined in the fight against the Soviets. The struggle for Ponyri began again. The Soviets directed their heaviest assaults against the XXXXI Panzer Corps, in an attempt to drive the Germans out of Ponyri. Although not evenly matched, the Germans proved determined to hold on to the area. Soviet attacks fell on the XXXXVI Panzer Corps and XXXXVII Panzer Corps as well. A

Above: 300mm (11.9in) rockets are loaded onto a Nebelwerfer ready to fire on Soviet positions in support of Model's troops. The trailer could be towed behind a light vehicle, making it fast moving.

Soviet thrust forced the XXIII Corps to relinquish Trossna, the village that the corps' formations had captured the day before. The Germans desperately fought back. Casualties mounted on both sides of the front as the fighting intensified. Unlike the campaign before 11 July, the Germans failed to launch a major attack in the Central Front sector. The 9th Army fought a strictly defensive battle. It was the Soviets who were on the move and who tried to break through the Germans' defences; however, Model was not yet ready to give up. Although the 9th Army's advances were non-existent on 11 July, the Soviets' successes were quite limited. As the fighting ended in the northern part of the Kursk bulge, neither side could claim even minor gains.

Soviet forces had failed to make major gains against a weary, understrength enemy. The Soviet commanders discussed the situation, especially the performance of the 2nd Tank Army. Between 5 and 11 July, the 2nd Tank Army, fighting alongside 13th Army forces, had repelled a large-scale offensive that the enemy had launched against the Orel–Kursk

axis. German formations had repeatedly pounded the Soviet defences. Entrenched within their powerful defences, the 2nd Tank Army and the 13th Army had crushed the armoured might of six German panzer divisions. Although the weight of the Tiger tanks and Ferdinand self-propelled guns fell on them, the Soviet defenders had yielded little ground. The equipment losses of the 2nd Tank Army and the XIX Tank Corps combined amounted to 46 per cent

Below: Nebelwerfer rockets are launched in a salvo from several launchers towards Soviet lines. The rockets were particularly useful in suppressing large area targets, as it was impossible to aim them accurately.

Above: A British-supplied Matilda tank in Soviet service that has suffered several hits from German shells on its turret. The Matilda was too slow and lightly armed to stand a chance against the latest tanks.

of the army's tanks. Soviet crews determined that approximately 49 per cent of the damaged tanks could not be repaired. Although Rokossovsky would have preferred territorial gains from the fighting on 11 July, he was satisfied that his Central Front forces had stopped the German advance and had possibly forced the Germans to shift to the defensive for the rest of the campaign.

On the night 11/12 July, Model again discussed the situation with Kluge. They had to make a decision about the strategy: whether to continue to

Below: A soldier takes advantage of a lull in the fighting to write some letters. Note the camouflage used to disguise his position. The machine gun in the foreground is a Czech weapon similar to the British Bren.

mount frontal assaults against the Soviet Central Front, or to regroup and try something else. Despite its performance through 11 July, Kluge was not willing to abandon the idea of the 9th Army achieving a breakthrough the next day. A ground situation report indicated that AGC had successfully repelled numerous Soviet armoured attacks south of Orel. The AGC commander assigned the 12th Panzer Division and the 36th Infantry Division to the XXXXVI Panzer Corps. Situated on the western part of the 9th Army's front, the XXXXVI Panzer Corps faced the Soviet 70th Army. With his sights set on a possible 12 July breakthrough and hoping to surprise the enemy, Kluge authorised a night attack on Ol'khovatka. The Soviet defenders in the town repelled the assault. As a result, the entire 9th Army maintained defensive positions for the rest of the night. Because the well-prepared attacks on 10 and 11 July failed to force the Soviets to retreat from the ridge south-west of Ol'khovatka, and because the night attack had also failed, Kluge agreed to send two more divisions – one infantry, the other panzer – to the 9th Army. Kluge argued that the two additional divisions would allow the 9th Army's next attack to succeed. Model consolidated his forces in preparation for a renewal of the Soviet assault in the morning.

Rokossovsky and Alexander Vasilevsky prepared for action in two areas: the Central Front area and the Orel bulge region. The two commanders had decided that the time had come to seize the initiative and the Orel salient offered excellent possibilities. The fierce fighting by the Central Front forces had tied down the 9th German Army. While the 9th Army was occupied, the Soviets' Western Front and Briansk Front forces could break through the enemy forces around Orel and then proceed south to get in position behind the 9th Army. Vasilevsky was just waiting for Stavka's orders to begin the prelude to the assault. Even before 5 July, the Briansk and Western front commanders had consolidated their forces for an assault on the German forces defending Orel. Commencement of the offensive, however, depended upon the struggle between the Central Front's and the 9th Army's forces. Stavka's assessment indicated that Soviet forces had sufficiently weakened and entangled the German Army, so Vasilevsky notified the commander of the Briansk Front, Colonel General Markian Popov, and the Western Front comander, Colonel General Vasily

Sokolovsky, that the time had come. Preparations for the offensive began during the night of 10 July, when a long-range bomber force attacked the enemy's rear. In the early afternoon of the next day, dive-bombers laid down smokescreens to protect Soviet reconnaissance battalions from the Western and Briansk Fronts as they probed the German defences at the northern edge of the Orel bulge. While Central Front troops engaged the 9th Army, other forces gathered information to facilitate another Soviet attack.

Rokossovsky and Vasilevsky discussed the results of the reconnaissance missions with Popov and Sokolovsky. As the Soviets prepared for a resumption of the fighting on 12 July, the Central Front's intelligence indicated that the Germans appeared to be regrouping their AGC forces and consolidating some of them farther north in the region opposite the Briansk Front area. Soviet intelligence noted the movement of German tank-, engineer-, artillery- and infantry units from the 9th Army's assault formations

Below: German tanks 'brewing up'. Model realised that his 9th Army could not resume the offensive; Rokossovsky and Vasilevsky prepared for a counter-attack in the Central Front and the Orel bulge.

Above: A Soviet T-34 after meeting an German anti-tank ditch unexpectedly, its barrel sunk deep into the soil. Its occupants would have been either stunned or knocked out by the force of the impact.

situation along the AGC front, especially in the 9th Army's and 2nd Panzer Army's sectors. From this, the German commander decided that a coordination of efforts in the two areas might succeed in bringing an operation that could develop into a major enemy offensive to a halt. Therefore, Kluge ordered Model to assume command of the 2nd Panzer Army. Model already had his hands full. Although the 9th Army could not renew its offensive on 12 July, that did not mean that its front was totally quiet. Vasilevsky and Rokossovsky intended to keep the Germans busy as the situation around Orel unfolded. The commanders wanted to hinder the transfer of forces from the 9th Army front to that of the 2nd Panzer Army.

The Soviet counter-attacks against the XXXXI Panzer Corps, which had begun early on 11 July, continued the next day. On 12 July, German artillery fire repelled three enemy thrusts. Soviet Stukas bombing the Germans near Ponyri set the surrounding forests ablaze. Smoke filled the air as the struggle between the two enemies intensified. As the German Nebelwerfers fired rockets at the enemy, the Soviets responded in kind with rockets shot from

Katyusha rocket-launchers. The Katyushas screamed as they fired volleys of approximately 48 rockets, which had a range of more than 50km (30 miles). The deafening noise increased as a Soviet cavalry formation charged the 110th German Armoured Reconnaissance Battalion. German machine-gun fire stopped the charge in its tracks. The cries from the mortally wounded horses no doubt added to the ever-increasing din.

The combination of Soviet assaults and Kluge's withdrawal of panzer- and infantry divisions and artillery all served to bring any further 9th Army advances to an end. At the end of eight days of hard fighting, the German 9th Army had penetrated less than 20km ($12^1/_2$ miles) into the Soviet line. The Germans' biggest penetration occurred at Teploe. After making their best gains during the first two days of the offensive, the 9th Army had failed to accomplish much more.

Kluge's transfer of panzer and infantry divisions from the Army Group Centre reserve force did not succeed in changing the course of the battle. This was because the Soviets' source of reserves vastly outnumbered that of their enemy. The Soviets appeared to be able to counter any reinforcements that the Germans introduced into the line. The struggle that began along the Orel salient on 12 July was just the beginning of what would later become a major Soviet offensive.

As they were planning Operation Citadel, the Germans realised that there was every possibility that the Soviets could attack them first. A particular area of concern in the Army Group Centre area was the Orel bulge. Of less concern at the time was the Kharkov salient in the Army Group South sector. The defences in these regions became increasingly weak as the Germans engaged in their preparations to launch Operation Citadel.

Of course, the Soviets recognised the increasing vulnerability of the German defences in these areas. In April and May, as Stavka prepared to meet the expected German attacks against the Kursk salient, the Soviet commanders also planned their own offensive operations. The Stavka commanders designed an impressive strategic summer offensive that consisted of a series of major counter-attacks.

According to the plan, the Soviets would launch one such assault, code-named Operation Kutuzov, directly against the Orel bulge. The course of the battle in the northern part of the Kursk salient would determine the target date for the beginning of Operation Kutuzov.

When the 9th German Army's attack stalled on 10 July, Stavka decided to finalise preparations for the commencement of Operation Kutuzov and issued the appropriate orders to the commanders of the Briansk and Western fronts. According to Stavka's orders, Briansk forces and those of the Western Front's left wing would attack on 12 July. At the same time, Rokossovsky's Central Front forces would continue to wear down the 9th Army. As the 9th Army should be sufficiently incapacitated within a few days, Rokossovsky's forces would join the attack against the Orel salient on 15 July. Therefore, the Soviet assault against the bulge on 12 July was not a final attempt to push the Germans back, but rather a prelude of what was to come.

Below: Soviet soldiers pose for a photograph in their British-supplied Universal Carrier, complete with a Bren Gun on an anti-aircraft mounting. One soldier is armed with an anti-tank rifle.

Armoured Clash

The Fight for Prokhorovka

Approximately 1400 tanks and assault guns met head to head near the town of Prokhorovka, in a battle that became a desperate, close range shoot-out which would decide the ultimate success or failure of Operation Citadel.

From the beginning of Operation Citadel, the 4th German Panzer Army had made greater penetrations into the Soviet defences than the 9th Army. The danger of a German breakthrough was more realistic in the southern part of the Kursk salient than it ever was on the northern shoulder. On the first day alone, the II SS Panzer Corps had advanced almost 20km (12^1/$_2$ miles) into the 6th Guards Army's defences and Army Detachment Kempf had formed a wedge 10–12km (6–7^1/$_2$ miles) wide and 3–4km (1^3/$_4$ to 2^1/$_2$ miles) deep into the 7th Guards Army's main line of resistance (MLR).

Despite the resistance of General Nikolai Vatutin's Voronezh Front, the Germans continued to push into the Soviet defences for the next few days. The II SS Panzer Corps had the greatest success in penetrating the enemy defences. Because of the defensive difficulties faced on the Voronezh Front, Stalin transferred the 27th Army to the region and approved the deployment of the 2nd Tank Corps and 10th Tank Corps to the Prokhorovka area. Vatutin's forces had to hold the line until the reinforcements arrived. For the next several days, as the Germans slowly pushed forwards and the Soviet defenders fought

Left: Hampered by smoke and enemy fire, Soviet artillerymen move a gun into position. Although they do not realise it, from the thick of the fighting they are about to witness one of the greatest tank battles in history.

feverishly as they withdrew, in order that they might have time to form new lines of defence.

According to the plan for Operation Citadel, the German forces were to advance an average of 20km ($12^1/_2$ miles) a day; however, Soviet resistance prevented that happening. Instead of having advanced 80km (50 miles) by the end of fighting on 9 July, the Germans' total movement after four days was only 20km ($12^1/_2$ miles). On the night 8/9 July, Stavka would make a number of crucial decisions designed to prevent an enemy breakthrough. The Soviet commanders decided to construct strong defences along the road leading to Oboian, which connected Belgorod and Kursk, and to continue the counterattacks against the Germans. Stavka issued orders transferring the Steppe Front's 5th Guards Tank Army to specified locations within the Voronezh Front region by 10 July. Once the tank army arrived, General Pavel Rotmistrov, following his orders from Stavka, deployed the forward elements along the Psel River and in areas west of Prokhorovka. Stavka also ordered the 5th Guards Army moved from the Steppe Front to the Voronezh Front and situated in

Below: German Tigers would play a main role in the armoured clash that would determine the outcome of the battle of Kursk. This Tiger belongs to the SS Das Reich *Division.*

the region along the Psel River between Oboian and Prokhorovka. According to his instructions from Stavka, General V. D. Kriuchenkin deployed the 69th Army to the area between the 6th and 7th Guards Armies in order to protect the Prokhorovka–Lipovyi Donetz River region.

As the Soviet forces moved into the positions designated by Stavka, Vatutin strengthened his defences, particularly along the Oboian road. He expected another enemy attack in the morning. The X Tank Corps and V Guards Tank Corps moved up to support the defensive efforts of General M. E. Katukov's 1st Tank Army. As the Soviet commanders carried out their preparations in the early morning hours of 9 July, the 4th Panzer Army commander, General Hermann Hoth, completed his plans for his next assault. Because of the previous days' successes, Hoth believed that forward elements of the XXXXVIII Panzer Corps and II SS Panzer Corps could break through the Soviet defences and reach Kursk, and they could possibly do it on 9 July. The Army Group South (AGS) commander, Field Marshal Erich von Manstein, promised maximum air support for the 4th Panzer Army's thrust against the Belgorod–Oboian highway axis.

At first, the Germans' 9 July advance went as planned. Forward elements of the II SS Panzer Corps

pushed through the III Soviet Mechanised Corps, which had already suffered great losses at the hands of the enemy, and proceeded towards Kochetovka. While the X Soviet Tank Corps prevented the Germans entering the town, II SS Panzer Corps divisions moved towards Prokhorovka. Repeated Soviet counter-attacks failed to stop the panzer corps. The V Soviet Guards Corps withdrew to establish a new defensive position in front of the advancing German panzers. While the II SS Panzer Corps headed for Prokhorovka, the full force of the XXXXVIII Panzer Corps' armour pushed northwards. Strong Soviet resistance, however, stopped it before the panzer corps entered its objective: the town of Novoselovkaon. Minor counter-attacks by the 1st Tank Army and the 6th Guards Army succeeded in limiting the XXXXVIII Panzer Corps' advance, but not in forcing the corps to retreat.

Further south, the III Panzer Corps of Army Detachment Kempf made little progress against the Soviet defences and failed to prevent the 5th Soviet Guards Tank Army linking up with the 1st Guards Tank Army. Although the Luftwaffe provided air support throughout the day, strong Soviet resistance

Above: A German soldier watches Soviet prisoners dig graves for their dead comrades in the shadow of a knocked-out T-34, its 76mm (3in) gun now pointing uselessly skywards.

prevented the 4th Panzer Army from reaching its main objectives on 9 July. This day marked the Germans' final major attempt at a frontal assault to break through the Soviet defences and advance to Oboian, from which they could launch an assault on Kursk. Despite massive armoured thrusts, the Germans only advanced 6–8km ($3^3/4$ to 5 miles) to the north as they lost almost 300 tanks and a large number of self-propelled guns, armoured transports and motor vehicles. Because the II SS Panzer Corps' advance had stalled outside Novoselovkaon, Hoth had altered his offensive plans and ordered it to shift direction and proceed directly to Prokhorovka. Hoth's decision would have critical consequences: a huge battle between the tanks of II SS Panzer Corps and the 5th Guards and 5th Guards Tank Armies, the likes of which had never been seen before.

As the Germans and the Soviets prepared to do battle on 10 July in the Voronezh Front's sector, the first American and British troops stepped foot on the

Right: Soldiers of the Waffen-SS wave to the camera as they prepare for battle on the back of a PzKpfw IV tank. All Waffen-SS troops wore camouflage smocks like these in battle.

southern coast of Sicily. Events in the Mediterranean caused the Führer to consider deploying his strategic reserves there at the expense of the campaign on the Eastern Front. Hitler even briefly contemplated transferring the II SS Panzer Corps to help meet the Allied threat on the Mediterranean Front, but the events unfolding in the Soviet Union delayed such a critical decision. Although AGS's progress on 10 July convinced Hitler to approve the continuation of the Citadel campaign, the 9th Army's failure to break through the Soviet defences north of Kursk and the Allied successes in Sicily eventually combined to bring an end to the Germans' summer offensive.

As had been the case since the beginning of the campaign, when fighting resumed on 10 July, it would occur in several areas in the salient south of

Kursk. South of Oboian, the XXXXVIII Panzer Corps hit the 1st Soviet Tank Army. North-east of Belgorod, the III Panzer Corps and the 7th Guards Army tangled. South-west of Prokhorovka, the II SS Panzer Corps locked horns with the 5th Guards Army and the 5th Guards Tank Army. Before the battle could resume, however, both the Soviets and the Germans had to move up reinforcements and supplies, and consolidate their forces.

During the night 9/10 July, General Katukov attempted to follow Vatutin's instructions for the 1st Tank Army's defences opposite the XXXXVIII Panzer Corps. He deployed the VI Tank Corps, commanded by General Getman, along the Pena River to protect the right flank of the 1st Tank Army. Supported by the 90th Guards Rifle Division and the III Mechanised Corps, both of which had suffered heavy losses at the hands of the Germans, elements of the VI Tank Corps faced east and south. Vatutin had transferred two fresh divisions – the 184th and the 204th Rifle Divisions – to protect the tank corps' rear. The combined strength of the VI Tank Corps was 100 tanks, but the X Tank Corps, with 120 tanks and self-propelled guns, had also situated itself to the rear of Getman's main defences. The weak III

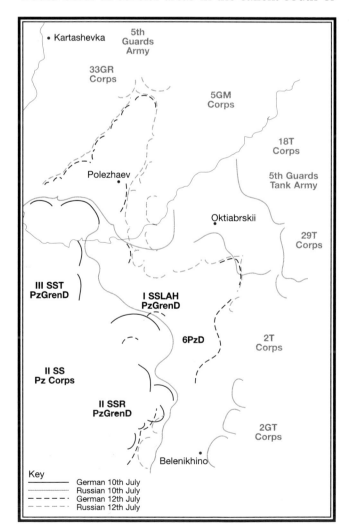

Left: German advances in the region west and south-west of Prokhorovka between 10 July and 12 July forced the Soviets to commit Konev's Steppe Front forces to the defence of the town.

Mechanised Corps, supported by 309th Rifle Division formations and V Guards Tank Corps, as well as anti-tank units, defended the Oboian road in the centre of the 1st Tank Army's line. On the army's left flank was the XXXI Tank Corps, which the 309th Division and the 51st Guards Rifle Division defended. Katukov had 300 tanks and self-propelled guns to protect the area between the Oboian road and the Psel River. Concerned about the 1st Tank Army, Vatutin moved the V Guards Tank and X Tank Corps and the 204th Rifle Division from his reserve to Katukov's control.

As Vatutin and Katukov regrouped, General Otto von Knobelsdorff prepared the XXXXVIII Panzer Corps for a thrust towards Oboian on 10 July. During the night, he concentrated his forces opposite a weak point in the Soviet line, the junction between Krivoshein's III Mechanised Corps and Getman's VI Tank Corps. Knobelsdorff planned a two-pronged attack. Concerned about an enemy threat to the corps' flank, he ordered the *Grossdeutschland* and the III Panzer divisions to hit the Soviet forces on his left flank, while the 11th Panzer Division initiated a thrust towards Oboian. Overly optimistic, the XXXXVIII Panzer Corps commander failed to realise the difficulty facing his forces. The fighting since 5 July had reduced his armoured strength to 173 tanks

and assault guns. Only 30 of the tanks left to him were Panthers.

The *Grossdeutschland* Division attacked at 0330 hours on 10 July. A bitter struggle raged in the groves and ravines in the area northwest of Verkhopen'e. The German division burst through the 200th Soviet Tank Brigade's defences, forcing Getman to shift formations of the 112th Tank and 6th Motorised Rifle brigades to his threatened left flank. In the pre-dawn mist, as the 60th Heavy Tank Regiment also moved up, confusion reigned in the Soviet line. The German division rolled through the Soviet defences and quickly captured the high ground of Hill 247, effectively cutting off the VI Tank Corps' communication line to the rear. The German advance separated the VI Tank Corps from the X Tank Corps, putting them both in danger. The battle intensified as the Soviets attempted to stop the Germans. The vicious fighting continued for another three hours before the *Grossdeutschland* Division, which suffered heavy losses, captured Hill 243. The badly mauled VI Tank Corps struggled against the German division throughout the day. Getman threw

Below: PzKpfw IIIs and IVs from 11th Panzer Division move forward in a column to attack Soviet positions. The fact the crewmen are exposed suggests that they are safe from attack for the moment.

reserves – the 200th Tank Brigade, the 6th Motorised Brigade and the 112th Tank Brigade – into the fight, but not as a unit. Consequently, the Germans ripped these brigades apart and almost destroyed them before they were able to retreat to safety under the cover of darkness.

Late in the day, the 3rd Panzer Division entered the battle. After following the *Grossdeutschland* Division through the town of Verkhopen'e, the 3rd Panzer Division turned south towards Berezovka and hit the defences of the VI Tank Corps. The III Panzer Division effectively knocked the Soviet tank corps out of the battle. By the end of a day of fierce fighting, the *Grossdeutschland* Division had advanced 5km (3 miles) north of Verkhopen'e to the town of Kalinovka. Despite the XXXXVIII Panzer Corps' successes of 10 July, Knobelsdorff notified Hoth of his concerns about the force's ability to achieve its objectives with its current strength. Hoth regrouped and provided the 3rd Panzer Division with additional infantry support.

On 11 July, the 3rd Panzer Division resumed its move to the south. With support from the 332nd Infantry Division, it drove the Soviet defenders out of

the Berezovka area. As it moved forwards, it pushed the 71st Guards Rifle Division west along the Pena River and advanced to the defences manned by the 184th Rifle Division, which extended south along the river. To counter the German thrusts, Vatutin deployed the X Tank Corps to the 1st Tank Army's right flank, where it was to strengthen the defences, as well as prepare to launch counter-attacks against the XXXXVIII Panzer Corps. Vatutin added the 219th Rifle Division to the X Tank Corps' position. Instructing Katukov to create a shock force capable of hitting and stopping the Germans, Vatutin placed all of the Soviet rifle forces in the area from the Psel River to the Pena River to the 6th Guards Army under Katukov's operational control. During the evening of 11 July, under General Hoth's direction, Knobelsdorff and General Paul Hausser, the commander of the II SS Panzer Corps, finalised their plans for a joint offensive scheduled to begin the next day, when the XXXXVIII and II SS Panzer Corps would begin a joint march on Prokhorovka. Hoth mistakenly believed that the Soviets had reached the end of their ready reserves and, therefore, that the enemy's position south of the Psel River was tenuous. The final drive to Kursk could begin the next day. To facilitate the drive, Hoth transferred the XXIV Panzer Corps from its reserve position to the Belgorod region.

Below: A platoon of Soviet T-34 tanks await orders to proceed to their assembly area for action at the front line. The camouflage on the first tank has wilted in the summer heat.

While the 3rd Panzer Division moved through the Berezovka region, the 11th Panzer Division slowly pushed its way against strong Soviet resistance. Although it managed to capture Hills 260.8 and 244.8, the panzer division failed to breach the Soviet defensive lines. By the end of the day, the division consolidated its positions from the Oboian road to the town of Kochetovka. During the night of 11 July, General Wietersheim of the 11th Panzer Division waited for the arrival of the *Grossdeutschland* Division, as he expected the two divisions to conduct a joint attack against Oboian.

From the outset, Field Marshal Erich von Manstein, the Army Group South (AGS) commander, had assigned Army Detachment Kempf the job of penetrating the 7th Soviet Guards Army's defences as it moved northwards and of protecting the right flank of the II SS Panzer Corps' advance towards Prokhorovka. For five days, Army Detachment Kempf had tried, but failed, to move deeply and quickly into the Soviet defences. By failing to do so, it could not protect the II SS Panzer Corps as it made its rapid advance. In addition, the nature of the III Panzer Corps's movements had left it exposed on both flanks. Soviet troops controlled a bulge that rested on the Northern Donetz and Lipovyi-Donetz rivers north and east of Belgorod. The Voronezh Front commander, Vatutin, noticing the vulnerability of the III Panzer Corps, issued new orders to General M. S. Shumilov. The 7th Guards Army should now continue to harass the flank of the German force east of the Northern Donetz, while at the same time preparing to launch a major counter-attack on 12

Above: Smoke billowing in the distance indicates where tanks have been knocked out by the Tigers that these Waffen-SS troops are accompanying forward to the battle.

July. To facilitate the 7th Guards Army's ability to fulfil its new orders, General V. D. Kriuchenkin and the 69th Army, with the addition of the XXXV Guards Rifle Corps, assumed the burden of maintaining the defences between Prokhorovka and Miasoedovo, in the region east of Belgorod. Kriuchenkin reinforced his defences as he prepared to stop III Panzer Corps.

On 10 July, as part of Army Detachment Kempf struggled to thwart attacks by the XXV Guards Corps and XXXV Guards Corps from the east, the III Panzer Corps attempted to resume its advance to the north. The 6th Panzer Division spearheaded the German movement. Three Soviet divisions – the 92nd Guards, the 94th Guards and the 305th Rifle Divisions – moved forwards to stop the panzer division near Melikhovo. By the end of the day, the 6th Panzer Division had lost more than half of its 100 tanks to Soviet anti-tank ditches, anti-tank guns, mines and artillery fire. Neither the 7th nor the 19th Panzer Divisions could provide the 6th Panzer Division with the support it needed. Although the Soviets had the 6th and 7th Panzer Divisions tied down around Melikhovo, the 19th Panzer Division began to push the Soviets back from the eastern bank of the Northern Donetz River. Kriuchenkin's decision on 10 July to shorten his lines to create reserves by withdrawing the 375th and 81st Guards Rifle Divisions allowed the 19th Panzer Division to make greater gains than it might otherwise have made.

Above: Mail call. Taking a break, these Soviet soldiers share the news from home. Many Red Army troops were illiterate, and relied on literate members of their squad to read and write their letters for them.

Late in the day, Werner Kempf gave in to pressure from Manstein and made plans for another attempt to break out east of the Northern Donetz River. During the night, the 7th Panzer Division quietly moved up and assumed the 6th Panzer Division's positions around Melikhovo. Kempf ordered the 6th Panzer Division to prepare for a joint operation with the 19th Panzer Division. Both divisions would move northwards along the eastern bank of the Northern Donetz River. With Tiger tanks leading the way, the 6th Panzer Division attacked at dawn on 11 July. The 19th Panzer Division pushed north along the left bank of the Northern Donetz River to Sabynino. The strength of the 6th Panzer Division thrust propelled it north 12km (7$\frac{1}{2}$ miles) and the division captured the town of Kazach'e. The mass of Tigers pierced a hole in the defences of the 305th Rifle Division and penetrated 10km (6 miles) into the rear of the 107th Rifle Division's line. While the commander of the

69th Army, Kriuchenkin, ordered the 81st Guards Rifle Division into the struggle to halt the German advance, the 89th Guards Rifle Division received orders to withdraw to a new defensive position. The 69th Army had held up Army Detachment Kempf for several days, but forward German units were only 25–30km (15$\frac{1}{2}$ to 18$\frac{1}{2}$ miles) from Prokhorovka. Although he strengthened his defences as much as possible, Kriuchenkin feared that his remaining reserves would be insufficient to prevent the enemy advancing further. Consequently, he requested help from Vatutin.

While the Soviet 69th Army struggled to contain the III Panzer Corps, Hausser's II SS Panzer Corps prepared to strike. Hausser's force had made the most gains from the AGS sector, but, as had been the case in other sections of the front, staunch Soviet resistance had slowed the corps' advance. During the night of 9 July, Hoth ordered Hausser to renew the fight the next day. Two SS panzergrenadier divisions – the *Totenkopf* on the left and the *Leibstandarte Adolf Hitler* on the right – moving on both sides of the Psel River would travel north-east and attack a series of targets – Prokhorovka, Hill 252.4, Hill 243.5 and Kartashevka – as they proceeded in that direction. Following an air and artillery barrage, the *Leibstandarte* Division would begin its movement at 0600 hours and capture its first targets: Prokhorovka and the high ground 2.5km (1^1/$_2$ miles) to the north-east, Hill 252.4. The *Das Reich* Division would seize the high ground to the southeast, while the *Totenkopf* Division advanced towards the northeast. Hausser issued the appropriate orders and the three divisions frantically moved towards their new concentration areas, from which they would launch their assaults.

Because of the difficulty in moving at night, the entire *Leibstandarte* Division had not yet reached its starting point by dawn but, in an attempt to fulfil Hausser's orders, attacked with its available units. Consequently, the *Leibstandarte*'s 10 July assault on Prokhorovka proceeded in a piecemeal fashion. Around dawn, a regiment of the *Totenkopf* Division crossed the Psel River and attempted to capture the high ground east of the Kliuchi village, Hill 226.6. The Soviet 52nd Guards Rifle Division and the 11th Rifle Brigade fiercely repelled the division. The *Totenkopf* Division had to seize the hill before it could continue its march to the north-east, which was timed with the *Das Reich* Division's thrust to the south-east; therefore, Hausser ordered a brief postponement. Poor road conditions caused further delays. The II SS Panzer Corps resumed its attack at 1045 hours. By noon, the *Totenkopf* Division crossed the Psel River and established a foothold. Brutal fighting for Hill 226.6 continued for the rest of the day, by which time a German regiment held the southern slopes of the hill and a small position east of Kliuchi.

Despite strong Soviet resistance, the *Leibstandarte* Division made good progress. Forward elements advanced through heavy Soviet tank and artillery fire and, by early afternoon, reached Hill 241.6, where a fierce battle ensued. The struggle for the hill continued throughout the afternoon in the midst of heavy thunderstorms; the Germans did not succeed in expelling the Soviet defenders until after dark. While suffering almost 200 casualties, the panzergrenadier division demolished more than 50 Soviet tanks and 20 anti-tank guns, but it failed to achieve its 10 July objective. The other II SS Panzer Corps divisions made limited gains. After a day of brutal fighting, the *Das Reich* Division finally captured part of a small

village south of the Prokhorovka road. The II SS Panzer Corps' slow progress did not discourage Hausser, who ordered renewed thrusts to Prokhorovka for the next day. He expected the last elements of the *Leibstandarte* Division to arrive in time to participate in the attack.

As Knobelsdorff and Hausser prepared the XXXXVIII Panzer Corps and the II SS Panzer Corps for an operation against Prokhorovka, Vatutin formulated careful plans aimed at stopping any German attacks by surrounding and destroying the main enemy concentrations advancing on Oboian and Prokhorovka. Having scheduled the offensive for 12 July, he was aware of the weakened state of the VI Tank Corps, as well as that of his tank army. Consequently, he gave Katukov new orders to regroup the Voronezh Front forces both to contain the enemy thrust and to form shock groups capable of conducting two major counter-attacks. With the

Below: PzKpfw IV tanks from the Totenkopf *Division negotiate a ditch on their way to the front line. The* Totenkopf *was initially held in reserve during the attack on Prokhorovka.*

Above: Even though they were particularly vulnerable to enemy fighters due to their slow speed, Stukas were successfully used as anti-tank aircraft when fitted with a 37mm (1.47in) gun under each wing.

reorganisation, the V Guards Tank Corps moved to the rear of the 184th Rifle Division, while the X Tank Corps formed an attack group with the 219th Rifle Division. What was left of the VI Tank Corps transferred behind the 184th Rifle Division in order to support the V Guards and X Tanks Corps' attack against the XXXXVIII Panzer Corps. The three tank corps together created a shock force of approximately 200 tanks. Vatutin deployed his remaining force – which included 150 tanks and parts of the 204th Rifle Division, 309th Rifle Division, III Mechanised Corps and XXXI Tank Corps – to the area from the Psel River to the region west of the Oboian road. He ordered these formations to assume a defensive position, but they would become part of the counter-attack if the enemy tried to withdraw to the south. In addition, two of the 5th Guards Army's corps moved up to the Psel River in order to support

the counter-attacks. Vatutin's counter-assaults would play an important role in denying the *Grossdeutschland* Division's participation in the Germans' main attack on Oboian and Kursk, which contributed to the outcome of events at Prokhorovka and Citadel's overall failure.

During the night, Vatutin evaluated the situation on the Voronezh Front and concluded that the Germans were regrouping for an assault along the Prokhorovka axis the next day. He informed Stalin about the possibility of an imminent enemy attack against this position. Although he believed that the main target would be the town itself, Vatutin did not rule out the possibility of further enemy action along the Oboian axis, as well as against the 69th Army. The Voronezh Front commander prepared his forces for the expected enemy assault. The II SS Panzer Corps' attack had caught the Soviets off-guard. Soviet forces had still been in the midst of regrouping for their 12 July attack. Vatutin did not want to be caught by surprise again; he intended to be prepared when the fighting resumed on 11 July.

The Germans had inflicted heavy damages on the II Tank Corps, which protected Prokhorovka. Vatutin therefore ordered the 9th Guards Airborne Division to reinforce General A. F. Popov's corps. By daybreak, the airborne division had established their defensive positions at the edge of the city's eastern suburbs behind the II Tank Corps. Three other divisions moved into the line – the 33rd, 95th and 97th Guards Rifle Divisions – to help stop the II SS Panzer Corps. The 42nd Guards Rifle Division, which was prepared to back up the 9th Guards Airborne Division or the 97th Guards Rifle Division, remained in reserve. Vatutin had an unplayed ace. On 9 July, the Voronezh Front commander had ordered General P. A. Rotmistrov to transfer the 5th Guards Tank Army from the Steppe Front sector into the Prokhorovka area. Within 24 hours, the powerful tank army had travelled 100km (60 miles) into the assembly area behind General L. S. Zhadov's 5th Guards Army. The 69th Army's General Kriuchenkin assumed control of Rotmistrov's force on 10 July.

To further strengthen the 5th Guards Tank Army, Vatutin provided reinforcements: the II Tank and II Guards Tank Corps, the 1529th Self-propelled, 522nd and 148th Howitzer, and 148th and 93rd Gun Artillery regiments, and the 16th and 80th Rearguards Mortar regiments. Rotmistrov had but a day in which to prepare for the offensive that the 5th Guards Tank Army, the 2nd Tank Army, and the 5th Guards Army

Above: An SS Tiger thrusts forward during the attack of II SS Panzer Corps. The tank has just successfully killed an enemy target using the long range of its 88mm (3.45in) gun.

would launch to the south-west of Prokhorovka with the start date of 12 July.

When the II SS Panzer Corps resumed its push for Prokhorovka early on 11 July, the Soviet forces had reached their new positions, but Vatutin had not yet completed the preparations for the counter-attack. Supporting the panzer corps' thrust, the Luftwaffe launched a massive air assault against the Soviet defences. The *Totenkopf* Division was to face heavy resistance as it tried to expand its foothold on the

Below: An exploding shell causes Soviet anti-tank gunners to flinch. In some parts of the battlefield cover was very sparse and troops and equipment could be very exposed to enemy fire.

Above: Entrenched SS soldiers look out over the scarred Russian countryside that stretches before them. Knocked-out Soviet tanks litter the ground in front of their position.

Below: A chance to snatch some rest despite the din of battle; this SS soldier is so exhausted from combat that he is content to use a 'Teller' anti-tank mine as his pillow.

southern slopes of Hill 226.6. Moving down from Hill 241.6, the *Leibstandarte* Division moved along both sides of the road to Prokhorovka; a *Das Reich* regiment protected the division's right flank. A Soviet tank brigade targeted tank and anti-tank fire on the German battalions leading the eastward advance. The battalions pushed their way forwards over 2km (1¼ miles) in less than two hours, as Soviet forces fired on their flanks and shells from the artillery guns located in Prelestnoe and Petrovka landed in their midst. Soviet troops dug in around Hill 252.4 opened devastating fire on the Germans and finally stopped their advance. A call for help resulted in the commitment of a panzergrenadier regiment that arrived with four Tiger tanks. German artillery opened up on the Soviet defenders and Stuka dive-bombers arrived on the scene. The Stukas began the hourly bombing of Soviet positions.

When the *Leibstandarte* Division renewed the attack at 0905 hours, it ran into the entrenched 9th Guards Airborne Division. Supporting Colonel Sazonov's airborne division were the remaining 169th Tank Brigade and the 57th Tank Regiment tanks, as well as the 5th Guards Army's 301st Anti-Tank Artillery Regiment. The fighting intensified.

Above: An SS machine gunner uses the burnt-out remains of a lorry as cover during the fighting. In the background lies another destroyed T-34, its turret hatches open.

Two of Sazonov's airborne regiments blocked the southern approaches to Prokhorovka and the 5th Guards Tank Army's assembly area. The airborne troops found the noise of the battle deafening as it slowly neared their positions. Sazonov unleashed his artillery at the approaching II SS Panzer Corps. Soon all the troops could hear was the sound of the artillery guns firing and shells bursting. A thick haze hung in the air, obstructing the view of the approaching battle. Everything seemed to be in slow motion. By 0950 hours, as the forward elements of the *Leibstandarte* moved towards Hill 252.2, they encountered the 26th Guards Airborne Regiment's concentrated fire. The battle for the hill raged for three hours and still the Soviet airborne troops held on. Although the *Leibstandarte*'s panzer group arrived at 1015 hours, the division did not seize Hill 252.2 until 1310 hours. Feeling confident in its success, the German division hurried down the western slopes of the hill towards a state farm. As the Germans descended the hill, Soviet artillery batteries

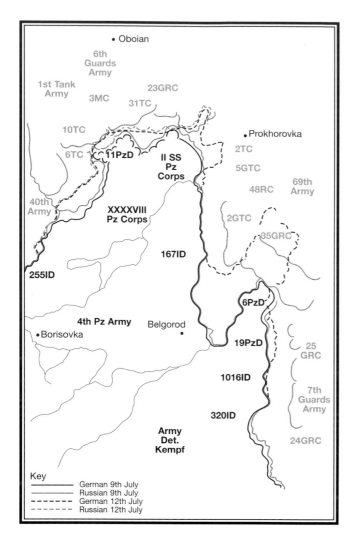

Key
—————— German 9th July
·········· Russian 9th July
– – – – – German 12th July
- - - - - Russian 12th July

Below: SS tank crewmen hurriedly grab more shells to load into their Tiger. During the intense fighting around Prokhorovka, running out of ammunition would prove to be a fatal predicament.

opened up furious anti-tank and direct fire. The brutal fighting continued and the Germans slowly captured the state farm. For the rest of the day, Soviet troops repeatedly attacked the panzer and panzergrenadier regiments that occupied the area. A real threat to the *Leibstandarte* Division's left flank developed when the 95th Soviet Guards Rifle Division joined the counter-attacks of the 99th Tank Brigade. By the end of the day, the German division found itself in a tenuous situation as Soviet artillery fire focused on its exposed flanks.

Although the *Leibstandarte* Division did not break through the Soviet defences, its advance forced a change in the Soviets' plans for 12 July. The German panzer division's pounding damaged the defences of the II Tank Corps beyond repair. In addition, it separated the 99th Tank Brigade from the rest of the II Tank Corps into the Psel valley. The forward movement of the *Leibstandarte* Division also caused a wedge to develop between the 95th Guards Division and the 9th Guards Airborne Division. Another German thrust created a salient deep into the defences of the 9th Guards Airborne Division close to Prokhorovka. Most importantly, the strength and distance of the German attacks of 11 July succeeded in boxing in many of the Soviet armies, including the 1st Tank, the 6th Guards, the 7th Guards and the 5th Guards Tank Armies. This forced a change to be made in the Soviets' counter-attack plans. The 5th Guards Tank Army, commanded by Rotmistrov, would be forced to assume the responsibility for carrying out the brunt of the attack, which was scheduled to begin at dawn.

Because of the weight of the German attack towards Prokhorovka, 11 July was not a particularly good day for Vatutin and the Central Front forces. Concerned about the deep penetrations made by the Germans into the Soviet defences, Stalin decided to place Marshal Georgi Zhukov and Marshal Alexander Vasilevsky directly in charge of the defence of Prokhorovka. Although the German threat to Prokhorovka hindered preparations for Vatutin's 12 July counter-attack, Vasilevsky approved the plan. Zhukov immediately got to work on plans to increase the odds of success. He grouped 10 artillery regiments into 'tank fists' and concentrated

them around Prokhorovka. These 'tank fists' had to help hold the columns of advancing Germans. Both the 5th Guards Tank Army and the 5th Guards Army, commanded by A. S. Zhadov, would fight damaging defensive battles while they prepared to mount the counter-attack. The 5th Guards Army defended the Oboian–Prokhorovka line.

The Soviets would face one of their most serious challenges of the battle of Kursk on 12 July at Prokhorovka, when their tanks clashed with those of the Germans. The Germans brought almost 100 Tiger tanks to the field, while the Soviets relied on the T-34. During the night 11/12 July, both sides finalised their preparations for the next day. According to Hausser's orders for the II SS Panzer Corps, the *Totenkopf* Division was to gain control of the rest of Hill 226.6 before advancing along the ridge to cut the Prokhorovka–Oboian road. The *Leibstandarte* Division received orders to continue towards Prokhorovka and seize the town and the nearby high ground, Hill 252.4. Both the *Das Reich* Division and the III Panzer Corps were to provide support. The AGS commander, Manstein, expected Hausser to coincide his attack with that of the

Above: Seemingly oblivious to the danger of approaching shells and bullets, so focused are they on the task ahead of them, Soviet ground troops support their tanks as they move into battle.

XXXXVIII Panzer Corps, which had orders to seize key Psel River crossings south of Oboian. After the two panzer corps had accomplished their goals, the Germans could successfully complete the move to Oboian and Kursk. Victory, from the south at least, was in sight.

Naturally, a German victory would not be easy. Vasilevsky, Vatutin and Rotmistrov were determined to seize the victory from the Germans' grasp. During the night, General A. S. Burdeiny consolidated the remaining 120 tanks of the II Guards Tank Corps into new assembly areas. Three of the corps' tank brigades would lead an attack against the *Das Reich* forces. To protect the flanks of the shock groups, Rotmistrov deployed two weak II Tank Corps brigades between the II Guards Tank Corps and XXIX Guards Tank Corps. He also moved up his reserve 53rd Guards Tank Regiment, along with 21 KV heavy tanks. To prepare for any eventuality, Rotmistrov placed the V Guards Mechanised Corps'

Below: Although the battle is obscured from his sight, a German soldier cautiously advances towards the sounds of fighting, while another soldier provides covering fire from his trench.

Above: A Soviet crewman proudly stands in front of his tank, the ubiquitous T-34. Fighting inside the tank was hellish – it was hot, cramped and very uncomfortable.

228 tanks and self-propelled guns in reserve east of Prokhorovka. Vatutin assigned artillery, mortar and anti-aircraft formations to Rotmistrov. In the initial assault, Rotmistrov would commit 430 tanks and self-propelled guns. He placed another 70 in the second echelon following behind.

Vatutin ordered Rotmistrov to begin the counter-attack towards the Komsomolets State Farm and Prokhorovka at 1000 hours. In conjunction with the 5th Guards Army and the 1st Tank Army, the 5th Guards Tank Army was to eliminate the Germans in the region and not allow an enemy withdrawal to the south. While Rotmistrov's 5th Guards Tank Army would launch the main counter-blow, Vatutin planned a counter-attack against the XXXXVIII Panzer Corps. Believing that the Germans would resume the offensive early on 12 July, Rotmistrov decided to move his target time up to 0830 hours; he issued the necessary orders. Most of Rotmistrov's forces had finished their preparations for the attack by 0200 hours on 12 July. Two hours later, however, Vatutin ordered a change. Army Detachment Kempf had pushed through the line in the south and had advanced to within 20km (12^1/$_2$ miles) of Prokhorovka. Rotmistrov received orders to send his reserve to help stop the Germans. Vatutin and Rotmistrov nervously awaited dawn.

Shortly after first light, Hausser's II SS Panzer Corps attacked. Within hours, however, the Soviet counter-attack would embroil corps' panzers and panzergrenadiers across the front in a fiery confrontation. At 0630 hours, the first German Messerschmitts arrived over the battlefield and, within a half an hour, German aircraft began bombing the Soviet defences. A short time later, Soviet fighters and bombers appeared on the scene. As one battle raged in the air, another began on the ground. At 0650 hours, forward elements of the *Leibstandarte* Division pushed the remaining Soviet defenders from the village of Storozhevoe. The division's target was Iamki, which was 2km (1^1/$_4$ miles) south-west of Prokhorovka. Before 0800 hours, the 2nd SS Panzergrenadier Regiment started down Hill 252.2 towards a state farm. The regiment quickly reached the ridge north of the farm, and as it fought against an enemy regiment and climbed the ridge, it received reports of a concentration of Soviet tanks positioned on the next ridge. When the panzergrenadiers – supported by an SS panzer regiment with Tiger tanks – started down the other side of the ridge, they began to notice the Soviet tanks. At first

they only saw a few, but soon more T-34 tanks than they could count were racing towards them, all carrying infantry. The panzergrenadiers and Tigers were about to lock horns with the 31st and 32nd Tank brigades of the XXIX Soviet Tank Corps. In addition, a 60-tank force appeared on the panzer regiment's left flank. With guns blazing, the two tank forces clashed. The battle, fought among burning tanks at close range, raged for three hours amid thickening haze and deafening roars. Despite their heavy losses, the two Soviet tank brigades, with the support of two XVIII Tank Corps brigades, slowly forced the panzer regiment to retreat. The fighting continued into the afternoon.

About an hour after first German formations began to attack, Soviet artillery opened fire, signalling the commencement of Vatutin's plan for 12 July. Following 15 minutes of Katyusha rocket fire, Soviet gunners shifted their focus from attacking German positions to protecting the advancing Soviet force. Shortly after 0830 hours, a mass of tanks and self-propelled guns, carrying 9th Guards Airborne Division riflemen, went into action. Rotmistrov's 5th Guards Tank Army counterattacked and ferocious tank battles erupted along the entire II SS Panzer Corps front. Particularly vicious fighting ensued in the *Leibstandarte* Division's sector. As the battles

Below: German Tiger tanks spearheaded the attack towards Prokhorovka. More than 500 German armoured vehicles were directed to attack the eastern flank of the Kursk bulge.

Above: Two German PzKpfw V Panthers knocked-out by the Red Army. The fact that neither has any hatches open implies that both crews were killed instantly.

intensified, the tank casualties increased. The attacking Soviet tanks suffered heavy losses. The tanks struggled to manoeuvre around the smouldering carcasses while keeping their prey within their sights. The fighting along the front grew in intensity as the day went on and it was to continue well into the afternoon before it finally died down.

Similar scenes played out all along the front. One wave after another of Soviet tanks pummelled the II SS Panzer Corps' forward units. Soviet forces from Bakharov's XVIII Tank Corps forced the attacking *Totenkopf* Division back to the west; as they pushed into the village of Vasil'evka, they almost cut the German division's communications with the *Leibstandarte* Division. The attack by General Kirichenko's XXIX Tank Corps on the main force of the *Leibstandarte* Division resulted in fewer gains and more casualties.

In a day of intense conflict, the fiercest struggle occurred on the XXIX Tank Corps' front. The 25th Tank Brigade, along with the 1446th Self-propelled

Artillery Regiment and the 28th Guards Airborne Regiment, broke through the German defences at Storozhevoe. Arriving at the Prokhorovka road, the tank brigade drove the 2nd SS Panzergrenadier Regiment back into the village. The Germans and Soviets brutally struggled in the town, on the southern slopes of Hill 252.2 and west of Iamki. Infantry-supported tanks attacked and then counterattacked, while artillery and anti-tank guns fired shells into their midst. Although Kirichenko's tank corps did not advance any further, its achievement was notable, in that it would prevent the forward elements of the II SS Panzer Corps from reaching Prokhorovka.

By the middle of the afternoon, the tank battles in the sectors of the XVIII Tank Corps and XIX Tank Corps had ended. Both the German and the Soviet forces were exhausted after a day of extremely ferocious and costly fighting. While the Soviets lost almost 200 tanks in one day of fighting, the German tank losses were fewer than half of those committed. Although Rotmistrov's 5th Guards Tank Army had thwarted the German attack on Prokhorovka, it faced a threat from the *Totenkopf* Division, which massed 121 tanks and assault guns north of the Psel River. The tanks, supported by the 6th SS

Panzergrenadier Regiment Eicke, hit the Soviet defences on Hill 226.6. Counter-attacks halted the German division, but the threat to the 5th Guards Tank Army remained. However, this was something that would have to be addressed the next day.

On 10 July II SS Panzer Corps tanks and assault guns had numbered a total of 300, while those vehicles which belonged to Army Detachment Kempf's III Panzer Crops were fewer than 200. The five corps of Rotmistrov's 5th Guards Tank Army posessed 830 tanks and self-propelled guns between them. The armour of the XXXXVIII Panzer Corps and the 1st Soviet Tank Army combined brought the number of combat vehicles which were concentrated along the southern flank of the Kursk bulge to a total of fewer than 2000.

Out on the battlefield, approximately 1250 armoured vehicles clashed along the eastern flank of the bulge, while more than 570 armoured vehicles struggled at Prokhorovka. The disorganised nature of the fighting at Prokhorovka was reflected in the very piecemeal fashion that both the German and the Soviet commanders were able to commit their forces to the battle.

As 12 July came to an end, Rotmistrov was forced to face certain undeniable realities. The 5th Guards Tank Army had managed to divert the enemy attack on Prokhorovka, but the unit had failed to stop the Germans' advance altogether. The XVIII Tank Corps and the XIX Tank Corps had borne the brunt of the fighting and suffered the consequences of it. They had survived, but between them these two units had perhaps, at the best estimate, 200 tanks with which to resume the fight the next day.

Accordingly, Rotmistrov ordered the commanders of these corps, Bakhorov and Kirichenko, to set about constructing strong defences. They were also instructed to withdraw their weakest units back to the second echelon.

As the remaining vehicles were re-loading with fuel and ammunition, Vatutin was engaged in rushing tank replacements to Rotmistrov. Throughout the evening, preparations continued, and Rotmistrov contemplated his plans for 13 July.

Below: Two German soldiers pose in front of their dug out, formed by the remains of two T-34 tanks. The force required to lift a T-34 suggests that they were destroyed by air attack.

CHAPTER NINE

The Soviet Riposte
The End of Citadel?

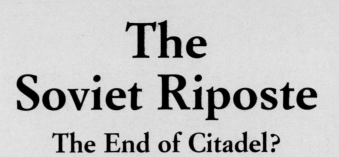

Despite limited success in the south, Citadel had clearly failed to achieve its objectives. With the Red Army launching its own attack in the north, and the Allies landing in Sicily, Hitler had to decide the offensive's fate.

As 12 July drew to a close, a tense situation existed throughout the front lines of the Kursk salient. It had been a day of thrusts and counter-attacks, a day of air and tank battles, a day of heavy casualties. It had been a day in which the 4th German Panzer Army had tried to break through the enemy's defences and reach Kursk, but it had also been a day in which the Soviet forces had fiercely fought to prevent this happening. The Soviets launched major counter-attacks beginning on 12 July, and continued for the next few days. The tide had begun to turn. Despite heavy losses, Soviet forces would hit the Germans again and again and again. When 13 July dawned, it would bring a new day of fighting; more importantly, however, it would bring decisions that would have major consequences for the Germans and the Soviets.

Soviet and Germans troops clashed in both the northern and southern parts of the bulge. The fighting occurred in two different areas in the Voronezh Front's sector. The XXXXVIII Panzer Corps and II SS Panzer Corps of the 4th Panzer Army struggled against the 5th Guards and 5th Guards Tank Armies in an effort to reach

Left: On 12 July the tide began to turn as Soviet forces to the south again thwarted a German thrust. In the meantime, the situation heated up in the north when Soviet troops began a counter-offensive against the Orel bulge.

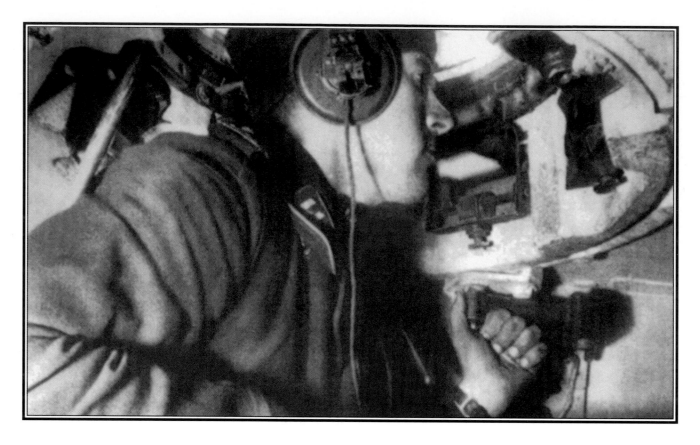

Above: A young SS tank commander views the battlefield through his periscopes. In cramped conditions like this thousands of young men fought and died on the battlefields of Kursk.

Prokhorovka from the south-west, while Army Detachment Kempf's III Panzer Corps took on the 7th Guards and 69th Armies. On 11 July, the three divisions of the III Panzer Corps continued their march north. Because the Soviets were retreating, the 19th Panzer Division made good progress, advanced 15km (9¼ miles) along the Northern Donetz River. Further to the east, the 6th Panzer Division broke through the Soviet line and forced the 305th Guards Rifle and the 92nd Guards Rifle Divisions to withdraw 15km (9¼ miles) to Rzhavets. The 7th Panzer Division burst through the Soviet defences at Schliachovo, as it struggled to proceed northwards while protecting the 6th Panzer Division's right flank. The III Panzer Corps' advance stopped for the day with the 6th Panzer Division establishing the point position and the other two divisions providing flank protection. General Werner Kempf ordered the corps to prepare for a renewal of the advance towards Prokhorovka on 12 July.

During the first several days of the campaign, Army Detachment Kempf had inflicted heavy damages on the 69th Soviet Army as it moved north towards Prokhorovka. By 11 July, General V. D. Kriuchenkin, the 69th Army commander, was fighting a delaying action. Whenever possible, he withdrew weakened formations from the front line and deployed them in rear positions, where they constructed new defences. The Soviets' elaborate system of defences had slowed the III Panzer Corps' advance, but it had not stopped it. Because of his army's distressing losses, Kriuchenkin feared that the 69th Army would be unable to stop the German panzer corps when it resumed the fight on 12 July. During the evening, Kriuchenkin requested reinforcements from Nikolai Vatutin. The Voronezh Front commander contemplated his options and reported the situation to Stalin. At 0400 hours, Vatutin called General Pavel Rotmistrov, the commander of the 5th Guards Tank Army, with distressing news about the situation to the south. The Army Detachment Kempf's forward thrust had pierced the defences. The Germans' advance units, which had already reached Rzhavets on the Northern Donetz River, were approximately 20km (12½ miles) from Prokhorovka. Vatutin ordered Rotmistrov to transfer his reserve to the south immediately. The tank commander contacted General K. G. Trufanov and ordered him to proceed south with the reserve quickly. Once there, Trufanov had instructions to place the reserve in the path of the advancing German divisions.

Concerned about the III German Panzer Corps, Vatutin decided to plan an assault that would distract the enemy corps and prevent the continuation of its march on Prokhorovka. On the night 11/12 July, Vatutin issued new orders to General M.S. Shumilov, the commander of the 7th Guards Army. The next day, the 49th Rifle Corps would attack the right flank of Army Detachment Kempf in the region east of Razumnoe. If the assault went as planned, the III Panzer Corps would have to turn away from Prokhorovka and protect itself from being cut off from the rest of Army Detachment Kempf. On the morning of 12 July, as the III Panzer Corps resumed its movement, Kempf and the corps commander, General Hermann Breith, had one goal in mind: Prokhorovka. The III Panzer Corps commander issued instructions to his subordinates the night before. Breith ordered the forward 6th Panzer Division formations, with support from the 503rd Panzer Detachment Tiger tanks, to advance to the north quickly. He also identified their objectives: Rzhavets and key Northern Donetz River crossings. Breith ordered the 19th Panzer Division to advance along the river's southern bank, to capture Krivtsevo and to connect with the 6th Panzer Division at Rzhavets during the night. Early the next morning, the 19th Panzers would help the 6th Panzer Division cross the river. Under cover of darkness, as the Soviet forces regrouped, Breith personally led the German column to Rzhavets. The Germans caught the 92nd Guards Rifle Division and the 96th Tank Brigade as they were regrouping. After a brief scuffle, the Soviet formations continued their move to the east. Elements of the reserve 375th Rifle Division remained behind to stop the enemy column. First Kriuchenkin, then Vatutin, received a desperate call for help.

Despite the daring rush to Rzhavets during the night, Prokhorovka was still 15km ($9\frac{1}{4}$ miles) beyond the III Panzer Corps' grasp by the end of the day. Rzhavets was only one of the 6th Panzer Division's goals for 12 July. The bulk of the division moved farther east to assault the high ground near Aleksandrovka, an area that the Soviets fiercely defended. The Soviet resistance at Aleksandrovka forced the 6th Panzer Division to abandon its drive towards Prokhorovka and go instead to the town. The 19th Panzer Division remained in the bridgehead, but did not continue the move north. By late afternoon, Rotmistrov's reserves arrived and joined the battle against the 6th Panzer Division. The quick action taken by Vatutin and Rotmistrov prevented the III Panzer Corps from proceeding towards

Below: Entrenched German soldiers observe the effects of their artillery fire. Soon they will be locked in mortal combat with their enemy when the Soviet counter-strike begins in earnest.

July, the struggle along the Orel salient broke out again. In the Western Front's sector, Bagramian's 11th Guards Army attacked in conjunction with the 50th Army, which was commanded by General I. V. Boldin. By mid-afternoon, Butkov's I Tank Corps, followed by the 1st Guards Rifle Division, moved through the hole in the German defences that had been created by the 11th Guards Army the day before. At first, the I Tank Corps had difficulty moving forwards, but a short time later the I Tank Corps and V Tank Corps burst through the Germans' second line of defences. Once through the line, the pace of the two tank corps increased. By the end of the day, the Soviets had created a wedge in the German position that was 15km (9¼ miles) deep and 23km (14½ miles) wide. Although the 5th Panzer Division contested the Soviet advance, it could not stop it. Without fresh reinforcements, the northern flank's collapse was imminent. That night Model sent three panzer divisions – the 12th, 18th and 20th – to bolster the German defences.

Popov's Briansk Front forces failed to make dramatic advances against the tip of the Orel salient due to Rendulic's XXXV Army Corps' defences. The day before, when the 3rd and 63rd Armies attacked the junction between the 56th Infantry Division and

Below: Soviet troops march towards the front. Their relaxed posture indicates that they are making their way through a secure village which poses no no obvious enemy threat.

262nd Infantry Division, the column did not progress as planned; KV-1 heavy tanks without infantry support advanced into a minefield. The Germans then shelled the exposed enemy tanks with anti-tank guns. When fighting ceased on 12 July, the Soviets had lost 60 tanks and only breached the first line of Rendulic's defences.

However, fighting resumed the next day, and A.V. Gorbatov and V. I. Kolpakchi, the 3rd Army and 63rd Army commanders, threw their follow-up rifle divisions into the narrow breach. By midday, General Pankov received orders to send the 207 tanks of his I Guards Tank Corps through the gap. Throughout the day, casualties mounted, but the 3rd and 63rd Armies made little progress. Model sent some reinforcements to Rendulic, and during the night 13/14 July, Rendulic received two panzer divisions from the OKH reserve: the 2nd and the 8th Panzer Divisions. They met the I Guards Tank Corps when it renewed the attack on 14 July, and stopped the Soviet corps from making a major penetration forward into the German line.

As a result of the limited movement made by the 3rd and 63rd Armies, Popov repeatedly appealed to Stavka for control of the 3rd Guards Tank Army. Commanded by General Pavel Rybalko and possessing more than 700 tanks and self-propelled guns, this reserve force was situated behind the front. Late on 13 July, Popov received control of the powerful tank army, but Luftwaffe activity restricted its movement

to forced marches at night. After two nights, Rybalko's exhausted force was in position near the eastern end of the salient, but by that time, the opportunity for a breakthrough by the 3rd and 63rd Armies had passed and, giving in to Stavka's pressure, Popov re-routed 3rd Guards Tank Army's attack. Instead of attacking Orel from the north and west, Rybalko's tank army was to come from the south-west.

Rybalko analysed the situation before issuing new orders to the 3rd Guards Tank Army. A man of action, he decided that an attempt to take advantage of the 3rd and 63rd Armies' assaults on the German defences would take too long: Rendulic's forces were firmly entrenched. He therefore decided to punch a new hole in the enemy's line with his powerful armoured force. More than 470 of the army's tanks were T-34s; the self-propelled guns numbered 32. However, he had neither the artillery nor the engineers necessary for a frontal assault. In addition, two fresh panzer divisions, almost two full infantry divisions, and several Tigers and Ferdinands were defending the German line. However, determined as he was to achieve a breakthrough, Popov agreed to Rybalko's plan.

On the morning of 19 July, a Soviet long-range bomber group prepared a path for the 3rd Guards Tank Army's advance. Supported by the bombers and artillery, the XII and XV Tank Corps burst out of their positions at 1030 hours. Once over the Oleshen River, the two corps pushed against the enemy defenders. The Germans tried to stop them with air and tank attacks and although this resistance slowed the Soviet advance, the corps had travelled 12km (7½ miles) into the German position by the end of the day. For five days, Rybalko's army manoeuvred in and around the German defences, changing direction whenever they received new orders from Popov. By 25 July, the 3rd Guards Tank Army cut the Orel–Kursk railway line. Despite repeated efforts, Rybalko failed to find a weak spot in the German defences, and the ensuing battle of attrition took its toll on the Soviet attackers and German defenders.

While the Germans in the Orel salient struggled against attacks from the north and east, a new threat came from the south. According to Hitler's orders of 13 July, Model's goals in the Orel bulge were to stop the Soviet advances, and restore the front to its previous position. As the general discovered, he could not achieve either. Moreover, on 15 July, forces from

Above: Guards Lieutenant N. P. Borozdnov stands proudly in front of his T-34. His was to be the first tank to break into Orel during the Soviet offensive after Operation Citadel.

Rokossovsky's Central Front attacked the southern part of the salient and, although they made little progress in this area, forced Model to shift his forces in an attempt to contest another offensive. For a week, the Soviets exerted pressure in the area while the Germans desperately defended it. On 16 July, in an effort to prevent the collapse of the salient's defences, Model prepared for a new line of defences that would permit a slight retreat. On 20 July, Hitler sent him an order forbidding this. Model contacted Kluge, who persuaded the Führer to reconsider.

The next day, the 11th Army joined the 50th Guards Army and 11th Guards Army's attack against the northern shoulder of the Orel salient. On 22 July, Hitler approved an 'elastic defence', which allowed Model to begin to withdraw the 2nd Panzer Army. Hitler was now willing to accept limited withdrawals on the Eastern Front. His decision signalled the beginning of Germany's retreat westwards.

CHAPTER TEN

The Aftermath

German Failure in the East

The prospect of a second front in Italy drained the German forces on the Eastern Front of reserves, and never again would the once-mighty Wehrmacht be able to launch a major offensive in the East.

As the Soviet counter-attacks against the Orel salient progressed, events continued to unfold farther south in the Voronezh Front sector of the Kursk bulge. Although he informed Field Marshal Günther von Kluge and Field Marshal Erich von Manstein of his decision to cancel Operation Citadel, Hitler did agree to allow the Army Group South (AGS) commander continue the offensive in order to destroy the Soviets' operational reserves and prevent them initiating a summer offensive. As he had suggested to Hitler on 13 July, Manstein was confident that another push by the 4th Panzer Army and Army Detachment Kempf would result in a complete penetration of the Soviet defences. The road to Prokhorovka and Kursk would then be open. The prize was within the Germans' grasp.

When fighting ended in the southern part of the Kursk salient on 12 July, Army Detachment Kempf's III Panzer Corps was only 15km (9¼ miles) from Prokhorovka. The 11th Panzer Regiment of the 6th Panzer Division had launched a daring move, caught the enemy defenders off-guard and assaulted Rzhavets. The bulk of the panzer division had advanced towards Aleksandrovka, but

Left: While Soviet counter-attacks against the Orel salient progressed, the 4th Panzer Army and Army Detachment Kempf prepared a final blow, which Manstein thought would open the road to Prokhorovka and Kursk.

Above: Enemy aircraft providing ground support made the movement of troops, ammunition, equipment, and other supplies to the front lines extremely difficult. Burning vehicles provided further obstacles.

strong Soviet opposition tied down the division outside the town. Relinquishing its position to the 19th Panzer Division, the 11th Panzer Regiment turned towards Alexsandrovka. As soon as he received reports of the raid on Rzhavets, General Nikolai Vatutin instructed Lieutenant General Pavel Rotmistrov, the commander of the 5th Guards Army, to transfer his reserves on the endangered Northern Donetz River region. Within an hour, the reserves were preparing to remove, but by that time the enemy had captured Rzhavets. Rotmistrov put his deputy, General K. G. Trufanov, in charge of the reserve force, which commenced the march to the south. Late on 12 July, the advance units entered the battle. While one detachment joined an attack by the 92nd Guards Rifle Division and the 96th Tank Brigade against an enemy regiment near Aleksandrovka, other detachments assaulted other

enemy positions in the area. Soviet attacks prevented the 19th German Panzer Division from expanding a small bridgehead across the Northern Donetz River. Because of the rapid Soviet response, the III Panzer Corps failed to reach Prokhorovka on 12 July.

As the III Panzer Corps pushed against the enemy in one area, two corps of the 4th Panzer Army attacked Soviet defenders manning the line south of Oboian. According to General Hermann Hoth's plans for the army, a thrust to the north by the XXXXVIII Panzer Corps would coincide with the II SS Panzer Corps attack towards Prokhorovka. Vatutin planned a counter-attack to eliminate the enemy threat to both Oboian and Prokhorovka. At 0900 hours, M. E. Katukov's 1st Tank Army attacked. As other Soviet formations attacked the Germans, the 1st Tank Army slowly drove the XXXXVIII Panzer Corps' 3rd Panzer Division back to the outskirts of Verkhopen'e and Berezovka. Soviet attacks against the *Grossdeutschland* Panzergrenadier and the 2nd Panzer Divisions effectively stopped any forward movement by the XXXXVIII Panzer Corps on 12 July.

On the morning of 12 July, the II SS Panzer Corps' three divisions renewed the assault to the north and towards Prokhorovka. Only the *Totenkopf* Division achieved some success, creating a narrow salient north of the Psel River. Counter-attacks by Rotmistrov's 5th Guards Tank Army prevented the enemy's direct thrust towards Prokhorovka. When they resumed the offensive on 13 July, the Germans would again meet determined Soviet resistance.

Despite the failures of 12 July, the Germans would resume the fight the next day. The first week of the campaign had brought a huge number of human and materiel casualties. The fierceness of the struggle surprised both German and Soviet commanders. Exhausted front-line troops, experiencing extreme duress, refused to give up the fight. The sounds of battle reverberated as cries of the wounded filled the air. A battle-generated haze created surreal surroundings as the soldiers fought to survive. As Kluge and Manstein travelled to the *Wolfsschanze* (Wolf's Lair) to meet with the Führer on 13 July, the battle-weary protagonists returned to a fight that had degenerated into a stalemate, particularly along the Prokhorovka axis. To the south, Group Trufanov arrived to halt the III Panzer Corps' 12 July advance. Not wanting to stop short of its objective, the III Panzer Corps began to slug it out with Group Trufanov. To the west, the dazed XXXXVIII Panzer Corps prepared for another round of fighting. The situation on the front lines would foster decisions that would have enormous consequences.

For the Germans, it was up to the III Panzer Corps and the *Totenkopf* Division of the II SS Panzer Corps to save the day. The *Totenkopf* Division's previous penetration had created a narrow salient that stretched north of the Psel River. According to General Paul Hausser's plan for 13 July, the *Leibstandarte* and *Das Reich* Divisions would push forwards until they reached the outskirts of Prokhorovka. At that point, because of the threat to their flank by the *Totenkopf* Division's forward units, the Soviet defenders should decide to retreat from the city. Once the Soviets had begun to retreat, the II SS Panzer Corps could resume the attack in conjunction with the III Panzer Corps. This joint effort would restore momentum and propel the two corps forwards towards their objectives.

Vatutin and Rotmistrov took the *Totenkopf* threat seriously. The possibility of the III Panzer Corps advancing from the south also concerned them. The two commanders gave General Skvortsov two important tasks to be accomplished by the V Guards Mechanised Corps. Skvortsov issued orders for the 10th Mechanised Brigade and the 24th Guards Tank Brigade to attack with rifle forces and eliminate the threat from the *Totenkopf* Division. The general instructed the 11th Guards Mechanised Brigade and 12th Guards Mechanised Brigade to concentrate their

Below: Climbing over the remains of a shattered wall, Red Army soldiers quickly, but carefully, advance into the open, their weapons at the ready in case they meet with resistance.

161

forces with those of the 26th Guards Tank Brigade. The three brigades were to prevent the III Panzer Corps from advancing to the north.

The Soviet attacks began again on the morning of 13 July, as German units attempted to move forwards. The *Totenkopf* Division reached its first objective before feeling the full weight of the armoured brigades and being forced to withdraw to its initial position. Fierce Soviet fire forced advance units of the *Leibstandarte* Division to retreat shortly after they had started. Thrusts by the *Leibstandarte* and *Totenkopf* Divisions would fail to penetrate the Soviet defences. During the early afternoon, Hoth requested permission from Manstein to shift his attacks to the east. Manstein agreed and a new German attack

began, but again failed to reach its objective. Constant counter-attacks by the Soviets in the afternoon would force the II SS Panzer Corps divisions to retreat to the positions that they had occupied in the morning. The Germans suffered similar results in all sections of the front on 13 July. A fierce battle raged along the banks of the Northern Donetz River between the 6th and 19th Panzer Divisions of the III Panzer Corps and the two branches of Trufanov's reserve formation. Trufanov's left column attacked the panzer corps formations concentrated in a small bridgehead across the river; the other assaulted the enemy formations near Aleksandrovka, penetrating the enemy's line between that town and Vypolzovka. Although they suffered heavy casualties, Trufanov's forces stopped the 19th Panzer Division's movement north. The tide was turning in the Soviets' favour.

Following his meeting with Hitler, Manstein returned to the front disappointed but determined.

Below: With the Germans falling back, Soviet soldiers take a cigarette break behind a knocked-out StuG III, confident in the knowledge that they can smoke in peace, if only for a few minutes.

He was a man with a mission to inflict as many casualties on the enemy as possible, particularly along the 4th Panzer Army's and Army Detachment Kempf's fronts. For the next two days, the field marshal attempted to achieve this goal. The XXXXVIII Panzer Corps received orders to renew the attack to the north. By the morning of 14 July, the *Grossdeutschland* Division had completed preparations and had assembled across the Oboian road. Coordinating its offensive with the 3rd Panzer Division, the *Grossdeutschland* Division attacked the area protected by the V Guards Tank Corps and the X Tank Corps. The Germans savagely attacked the Soviet tank corps for two days and inflicted heavy damages on them, as well as on the VI Tank Corps, which had arrived to reinforce the two tank corps. Soviet rifle divisions, which supported the tank corps, suffered under the weight of the strong assaults. Soviet attempts at counter-blows to deflect the enemy thrusts failed. The German panzer divisions also forced the 6th Guards Army to retreat almost 2km (1¼ miles), and advance elements of the *Grossdeutschland* Division linked up with the 3rd Panzer Division near Berezovka. On 15 July, Vatutin ordered General Katukov to place the 1st Tank Army on the defensive. He instructed General I. M. Chistiakov and General A. S. Zhadov, the commanders of the 6th Guards Army and 5th Guards Army, respectively, to be prepared to assume control of the 1st Tank Army's sector. The readjustment of the Soviet defences on the XXXXVIII Panzer Corps front occurred by the night 16/17 July. Although the vulnerable 3rd Panzer Division had received support, the continuous fighting further weakened the *Grossdeutschland* Division. Despite the minor successes, the offensive of 14 July proved costly; only a few of the original 80 Panther tanks remained serviceable. The battle-weary 1st Tank Army had again denied the XXXXVIII Panzer Corps access to Kursk.

Manstein realised that the ability of the 4th Panzer Army and Army Detachment Kempf to continue Operation Citadel was diminishing, but the creation of a unbroken front line near Prokhorovka before all offensive operations ceased was important. On the evening of 13 July, General Hausser received new orders for the II SS Panzer Corps' next offensive, called Roland. While the *Totenkopf* Division firmly held its position, the *Das Reich* and *Leibstandarte* Divisions would attack. The *Leibstandarte* Division's assault would not begin until the *Das Reich*

Above: P. A. Rotmistrov (left), commander of the 5th Guards Tank Army, and A. S. Zhadov, commander of the 5th Guards Army, discuss events not far from Prokhorovka in July 1943.

Division's thrust had effectively commenced. In addition, Army Detachment Kempf was to initiate a cooperative action. General Hermann Breith, the III Panzer Corps commander, received instructions to concentrate the 7th and 19th Panzer Divisions' forces. The two divisions would attack to the north and north-west in order to connect with the *Das Reich* Division and eliminate the Soviet presence between the Lipovyi-Donetz and Northern Donetz rivers. The ultimate goal was the seizure of Prokhorovka. Follow-up elements of the 4th Panzer Army and Army Detachment Kempf would surround any remaining enemy forces and solidify the gains made by the divisions. The 6th Panzer Division would carry out assaults to provide flank support for the advancing divisions, as well as to eliminate the Soviet presence in Aleksandrovka.

As they had previously, Vatutin and Zhukov correctly guessed what the Germans would do next and made preparations to thwart the enemy. They transferred all of the available armoured reserves to help General Trufanov. The two commanders ordered two tank corps – the XVIII Tank Corps and XXIX Tank Corps – of the 5th Guards Tank Army to prevent the II SS Panzer Corps from reaching Prokhorovka. Despite the Soviets' preparations, the German attack threatened to surround five divisions of the 69th Army on 15 July. That evening, Vatutin instructed General V. D. Kriuchenkin to withdraw the endangered divisions, and their timely retreat prevented their encirclement.

Above: Relieved to be out of the front lines, these German soldiers march across a bridge and out of Orel to the rear, carrying their kit and weapons and covered in the grime of heavy combat.

The fighting on 14/15 July, the last days of Citadel, was as brutal as any throughout the campaign. Despite local successes, victory for the Germans was not possible. Advances on the northern and southern flanks had been insufficient to close the 130km (80 mile) gap, between the forces of Werner Kempf and Hermann Hoth, which contained entrenched Soviet troops, minefields, tanks and artillery. Although the end had come, the Germans continued the fight for the next few days. By 17 July, Manstein's forces had established a continuous front south of Prokhorovka, but the field marshal was unable to capitalise on this success. In fact, on 16 July, under cover of fire provided by rearguard forces, 4th Panzer Army and Army Detachment Kempf forces began to withdraw. The Führer's attention shifted away from the campaign in the Soviet Union to the military situation elsewhere. The *Afrika Korps* had lost the battle for North Africa. Hitler considered an invasion across the English Channel by Allied forces into German-occupied Northern Europe a real possibility. The Allies were winning the battle for Sicily and an Allied victory in Sicily spelled danger for Italy. Concerned about the Mediterranean theatre, Hitler ordered the II SS Panzer Corps removed from the Eastern Front and transferred south.

Although the German offensive effort had ended, that of the Soviets had not. Operation Kutuzov, the assault on the Orel salient that began on 12 July, was only one of the massive counter-attacks planned by the Soviets. Operation Kutuzov had done its job. It had siphoned off enemy troops from the Central Front's sector. A second large counter-offensive, with the code name Operation Rumiantsev, began a few weeks later. The Soviets planned to accomplish ambitious goals with this major counter-attack. While freeing Belgorod and Kharkov from enemy occupation was part of the plan, the main goal of Rumiantsev was the annihilation of two battle-weary German forces: the 4th Panzer Army and Army Detachment Kempf. The bitter fighting in the Voronezh Front sector, the transfer of German forces to the Orel salient and of the II SS Panzer Corps from the Eastern Front, and the commencement of a retreat of German forces weakened the 4th Panzer Army sufficiently for the counter-offensive to begin. As the Soviet attack developed, it would also involve the Kalinin, South-western and Southern front forces.

Although the members of Stavka had made the decision to implement Rumiantsev in April, they did not finalise the plans until the Battle for Kursk had run its course. Stalin favoured opening the offensive as early as 23 July, but Zhukov convinced him to wait until preparations for the offensive had been completed. On 24 July, General Vatutin and General Ivan Konev received orders from Stavka officials to complete final preparations for Rumiantsev. As the Soviets prepared, German intelligence indicated the westward movement of a large number of enemy troops. Consequently, Manstein ordered an organised withdrawal. For the rest of the month, troops, fuel, ammunition and equipment arrived at the assembly area. On 1 August, Stalin approved the final plan, which included a massive attack by several Voronezh and Steppe Front armies. Vatutin would supply two Voronezh Front armies – the 5th Guards Army commanded by General Zhadov and General Chistiakov's 6th Guards Army – for the attack. The Voronezh Front forces would be joined in the assault by three of Konev's armies – General Managarov's 53rd Army, the 69th Army commanded by Kriuchenkin and part of General M.S. Shumilov's 7th Guards Army. According to the plan, the five armies would hit German forces north and north-west of Belgorod. In conjunction with the attack at Belgorod, Katukov and Rotmistrov had orders to send the 1st Tank Army and the 5th Guards Tank

Army to the south-west. The tank armies would quickly seize Bogodukhov's rail and logistical centre before advancing to Kharkov and then surrounding the city.

On 3 August, the front exploded as Soviet artillery commenced an intense bombardment at 0500 hours. Shortly before 0800 hours, the guns began to target the enemy's rear positions as the tank-supported ground troops attacked. Within two hours, Soviet troops had penetrated the German defences. In the early afternoon, Vatutin ordered four brigades from the 1st Guards Tank Army and Fifth Guards Tank Army to move forwards. Although not all of the attacks against the enemy's front line achieved penetration, forward formations of the 1st and 5th Guards Tank Armies advanced 25km ($15\frac{1}{2}$ miles) into the German position, cutting the road between Belgorod and Tomarovka. Following the tank brigades, rifle formations advanced 8–10km (5–$6\frac{1}{4}$ miles). The fierceness of the Soviet attack surprised the German defenders and ripped a 10km ($6\frac{1}{4}$ mile) gap between the 4th Panzer Army and Army Detachment Kempf. During the brutal assault, the Soviets almost completely destroyed a regiment of the 167th Infantry Division while inflicting heavy

Below: Mesmerised by the burning buildings, men of a motorcycle combination unit pause near Orel before continuing their retreat in the face of the advancing Red Army.

SOVIET ORDER OF BATTLE
CENTRAL FRONT, 1 JULY 1943

13TH ARMY
17th, 18th Guards (Gds) Rifle Corps, 15th, 29th Rifle Corps

Army Troops
FIELD ARTILLERY
4th Breakthrough Artillery Corps, 5th, 12th Breakthrough Art. Div., 5th Gds Rocket Art.Div., 19th Gds Cannon Regt., 476th, 477th Mtr.Regt., 6th, 37th, 65th, 86th, 324th Gds Rocket Art.Regt.
OTHERS
275th Eng.Bn., 1st, 25th AA Div., 1287th AA Regt., 874th Anti-Tank (AT) Regt., 129th Tank Bde, 27th, 30th Gds Tank Regt., 43rd, 58th, 237th Tank Regt., 1442nd SU Regt., 49th Armoured (Armd) Train Bn.

48TH ARMY
42nd Rifle Corps, 73rd, 137th, 143rd, 170th Rifle Div.

Army Troops
FIELD ARTILLERY
1168th Cannon Regt., 479th Mtr.Regt.
OTHERS
313th Eng.Bn., 16th AA Div., 461st AA Regt., 615th AA Bn., 2nd AT Bde., 220th Gds AT Regt., 45th, 193rd, 229th Tank Regt., 1454th, 1455th, 1540th SU Regt., 37th Armd Train Bn.

60TH ARMY
24th, 30th Rifle Corps, 55th Rifle Div., 248th Rifle Bde

Army Troops
FIELD ARTILLERY
1156th Cannon Regt., 128th, 138th, 497th Mtr.Regt., 98th Gds Rocket Art.Regt., 286th Gds Rocket Art.Bn.
OTHERS
59th Eng.Sapper Bde, 317th Eng.Bn., 221st Gds AA Regt., 217th AA Regt., 1178th AT Regt., 150th Tank Bde, 58th Armd Train Bn.

65TH ARMY
18th, 27th Rifle Corps, 37th Gds Rifle Div., 181st, 194th, 354th Rifle Div.

Army Troops
FIELD ARTILLERY
143rd Gds Mtr.Regt., 218th, 478th Mtr.Regt., 94th Gds Rocket Art. Regt.
OTHERS
14th Eng.-Mine Bde., 321st Eng.Bn., 29th Gds Tank Regt., 40th, 84th, 255th Tank Regt., 120th, 543rd AT Regt., 235th AA Regt.

70TH ARMY
28th Rifle Corps, 102nd, 106th,

140th, 162nd, 175th (NKVD) Rifle Div.

Army Troops
FIELD ARTILLERY
1st Gds Art.Div., 136th Mtr.Regt.
OTHERS
169th, 371st, 386th Eng. Bn., 3rd Destroyer Bde., 240th, 251st, 259th Tank Regt., 378th AT Regt., 12th AA Div., 581st AA. Reg.

2ND TANK ARMY
3rd, 16th Tank Corps

Army Troops
OTHERS
357th Eng.Bn., 11th Gds Tank Bde., 87th MC Bn.

FRONT RESERVES
9th, 19th Tank Corps, 115th, 119th, 161st Fortified Sectors

Support Troops
FIELD ARTILLERY
68th Cannon Art.Bde., 21st Mtr. Bde., 84th, 92nd, 323rd Gds Rocket Art. Regt.
OTHERS
1st Gds Special Purposes Eng. Bde., 6th Mine Eng.Bde., 12th Gds Mine Bn., 120th, 257th Eng.Bn., 9th, 49th, 50th, 104th Pont. Bn., 1541st SU Regt., 4th Destroyer Bde., 14th Destroyer Bde., 40th Armd Train Bn., 1st AT Bde., 13th AT Bde., 130th, 563rd AT Regt., 10th AA Div., 997th, 325th, 1259th, 1263rd AA Regt., 13th Gds, 27th, 31st AA Bn.

VORONEZH FRONT, 1 JULY 1943

6TH GUARDS ARMY
22nd, 23rd Gds Rifle Corps, 89th Gds Rifle Div.

Army Troops
FIELD ARTILLERY
27th, 33rd Cannon Art.Bde., 628th Cannon Art.Regt., 263rd, 295th Mtr.Regt., 5th, 16th, 79th, 314th Gds Rocket Art.Regt.
OTHERS
205th, 540th Eng.Bn., 96th Tank Bde., 230th, 245th Tank Regt., 1440th SU Regt., 60th Armd Train Bn., 27th, 28th AT Bde., 493rd, 496th, 611th, 694th, 868th, 1008th, 1240th, 1666th, 1667th AT Regt., 26th AA Div., 1487th AA Regt.

7TH GUARDS ARMY
24th, 25th Gds Rifle Corps, 213th Rifle Div.

Army Troops
FIELD ARTILLERY
109th, 161st, 265th Gds Cannon Art.Regt., 290th Mtr.Regt.
OTHERS

60th Eng.Sapper Bde., 175th, 329th Eng.Bn., 27th Gds Tank Bde., 201st Tank Bde., 262nd, 148th, 167th Tank Regt., 1529th, 1438th SU Regt., 34th, 38th Armd Train Bn., 30th AT Bde., 114th, 115th Gds AT Regt., 1669th, 1670th AT Regt., 5th AA Div., 162nd, 258th Gds AA Regt.

38TH ARMY
167th, 180th, 204th, 232nd, 240th, 340th Rifle Div.

Army Troops
FIELD ARTILLERY
111th Gds How. Art. Regt., 112th Gds Cannon Art.Regt., 491st, 492nd Mtr.Regt., 66th Gds Rocket Art.Regt., 441st Gds Rocket Art.Bn
OTHERS
235th, 268th Eng.Bn., 1505th Mine Eng.Bn., 108th Pontoon Bn., 180th, 192nd Tank Bde., 29th AT Bde., 222nd, 483rd, 1658th, 1660th, 981st, 1288th AA Regt.

40TH ARMY
100th, 161st, 184th, 206th, 219th, 237th, 309th Rifle Div.

Army Troops
FIELD ARTILLERY
36th Cannon Art.Bde., 29th How. Art. Bde. (–), 76th Gds Cannon Art. Regt., 493rd, 494th Mtr. Regt., 9th, 10th Mtn. Mtr. Regt.
OTHERS
14th Eng.Bn., 86th Tank Bde., 59th, 60th Tank Regt., 32nd AT Bde., 4th Gds AT Regt., 12th, 869th, 1244th, 1663rd, 1664th AT Regt., 9th AA Div., 1488th AA Regt.

69TH ARMY
107th, 111th, 183rd, 270th, 305th Rifle Div.

Army Troops
FIELD ARTILLERY
496th Mtr.Regt.
OTHERS
328th Eng.Bn., 1661st AT Regt., 225th Gds AA Regt., 322nd AA Bn.

1ST TANK ARMY
3rd Mech. Corps, 6th, 31st Tank Corps

Army Troops
FIELD ARTILLERY
316th Gds Rocket Art.Regt.
OTHERS
71st, 267th Eng.Bn., 8th AA Div.

FRONT RESERVES
2nd, 5th Gds Tank Corps, 35th Gds Rifle Corps

Support Troops
FIELD ARTILLERY
1528th How.Art.Regt., 522nd, 1148th

Super Hvy.How.Art.Regt., 12th Mtr. Bde., 469th Mtr.Regt., 36th, 80th, 97th, 309th, 315th Gds Rocket Art. Regt.
OTHERS
4th, 5th Mine Eng.Bde., 42nd Special Purposes Eng.Bde., 6th Pontoon Bde., 13th Gds Mine Bn., 6th, 20th Pont. Bn., Separate Tank Regt. (unnumbered), 14th, 31st AT Bde., 1076th, 1689th AT Regt., 22nd Gds AA Bn.

STEPPE FRONT (STEPPE MILITARY DISTRICT), 1 JULY

4TH GUARDS ARMY
20th, 21st Gds Rifle Corps, 3rd Gds Tank Corps

Army Troops
FIELD ARTILLERY
466th Mtr.Regt., 96th Gds Rocket Art.Regt.
OTHERS
48th Eng.Bn., 452nd, 1317th AT Regt., 27th AA Div.

5TH GUARDS ARMY
32nd, 33rd Gds Rifle Corps, 10th Tank Corps, 42nd Gds Rifle Div.

Army Troops
FIELD ARTILLERY
308th Gds Rocket Art.Regt.
OTHERS
256th, 431st Eng.Bn., 301st, 1322nd AT Regt., 29th AA Div

27TH ARMY
71st, 147th, 155th, 163rd, 166th, 241st Rifle Div.

Army Troops
FIELD ARTILLERY
480th Mtr.Regt., 47th Gds Rocket Art.Regt.
OTHERS
25th, 38th Eng.Bn., 680th, 1070th AT Regt., 93rd Tank Bde., 39th Tank Regt., 23rd AA Div.

47TH ARMY
21st, 23rd Rifle Corps

Army Troops
FIELD ARTILLERY
460th Mtr. Regt., 83rd Gds Rocket Art.Regt.
OTHERS
91st Eng. Bn., 269th, 1593rd AT Regt., 21st AA Div

53RD ARMY
28th Gds, 84th, 116th, 214th, 233rd, 252nd, 299th Rifle Div.

Army Troops
FIELD ARTILLERY
461st Mtr. Regt., 89th Gds Rocket Art. Regt.
OTHERS

11th, 17th Eng. Bn., 232nd, 1316th AT Regt., 34th, 35th Tank Regt., 30th AA Div

5TH GUARDS TANK ARMY

5th Gds Mech. Corps, 29th Tank Corps

Army Troops

FIELD ARTILLERY

678th How.Art.Regt., 76th Gds Rocket Regt.

OTHERS

377th Eng.Bn., 994th Light Bomber Regiment, 689th AT Regt., 53rd Gds Tank Regt., 1549th SU Regt., 1st Gds MC Regt., 6th AA Div

FRONT RESERVES

35th Rifle Corps (HQ only), 3rd, 5th, 7th Gds Cavalry Corps, 4th Gds Tank Corps, 3rd Gds Mech. Corps, 1st, 2nd Mech. Corps

Support Troops

ENGINEERS

8th Eng.Sapper Bde., 27th Special Purposes Eng.Bde., 7th, 19th, 40th Pontoon Bn., 246th, 247th, 248th, 250th, 284th Eng.Bn.

OTHERS

78th MC Bn., 11th AA Div.

REINFORCEMENT FROM SOUTH-WESTERN FRONT

2nd Tank Corps

REINFORCEMENT FROM STAVKA RESERVES

18th Tank Corps

AIR ARMIES SUPPORTING THE SOVIET FORCES

2nd Air Army (Voronezh Front), 5th Air Army (Steppe Front), 16th Air Army (Central Front), 17th Air Army (Southwestern Front)

GERMAN ORDER OF BATTLE

4TH PANZER ARMY, 6 JULY 1943

LII CORPS

57th, 255th, 332nd Inf. Div.

Corps Troops

FIELD ARTILLERY

Arko 137, I/108th Field Art.Bn. (RSO), 3rd/731st 15cm Gun Battery, 1st Hvy.Rocket Art.Regt.

OTHERS

677th Eng.Regt., 74th Eng.Bn., 217th Constr.Bn., 23rd, 80th Bridge Column Bn., 226th Bicycle Security Bn. (minus 1 Coy.)

XXXXVIII PANZER CORPS

167th Inf. Div., 3rd, 11th Pz. Div. and *Großdeutschland* Pz.Gren. Div.

Corps Troops

FIELD ARTILLERY

Arko 132, 144, 70th Art.Regt.Staff, III/109th Howitzer Bn. (motorized

(m)), 101st Hvy.Field Art.Bn., 842nd 10cm Gun Bn., 911th Assault Gun Bn., 19th Lt.Art.Obsv.Bn.

OTHERS

515th Eng.Regt., 48th Eng.Bn. (m), 1st Eng. Training Bn., Bridging Staff 938, 81st Bridge Constr. Bn. (minus 4th Coy.), 616th Army AA Coy.

II SS-PANZER CORPS

SS-Totenkopf, SS-Das Reich and *SS-Leibstandarte* Pz. Gren. Div.

Corps Troops

FIELD ARTILLERY

Arko 122, 861st, III/818th Field Art.Bn. (RSO), Commander of Smoke Troops 3, 55th Rocket Art.Regt., 1st Lehr Rocket Art.Regt., SS-Corps Rocket Art Bn.

ENGINEERS

680th Eng.Regt., 627th, 666th Eng.Bn. (m), Bridging Staff 929, Commander of Constr. Troops 8., 26th Bridge Constr.Bn., 508th Lt.Bicycle Road Constr.Bn., 410th Constr.Bn.

Army Troops

Higher Arko 312, Higher Constr. Staff 14, Commander for Constr. Forces 14, 155th Constr.Bn. (K), 305th Const.Bn., Bridging Staff 922

ARMY DETACHMENT KEMPF, 4 JULY

III PANZER CORPS

168th Inf. Div., 6th, 7th, 19th Pz. Div.

Corps Troops

FIELD ARTILLERY

Arko 3, 612th Art.Regt., 857th 21cm How.Bn., II/62nd Field Art.Bn., II/71st Hvy.Field Art.Bn., 228th Assault Gun Bn., 54th Rocket Art. Regt.

OTHERS

601st, 674th Eng.Regt. (m), 70th, 651st Eng.Bn. (m), 127.Eng Bn. (m) (minus 1 Coy.), 531st, 925th Bridge Constr. Bn., 503rd Hvy Tank Bn., 99th, 153rd AA Regt.

RAUS CORPS

106th, 320th Inf. Div.

Corps Troops

FIELD ARTILLERY

Arko 153, I/77th, I/213th, II/54th Field Art.Bn., 31st Lt.Art.Obsv.Bn., 905th Assault Gun Bn., 393rd Assault Gun Battery, II/1st Hvy.Rocket-Launcher Regt., 52nd Rocket Art. Regt.

OTHERS

18th, 52nd Eng.Bn. (m), 923rd, 41st Bridge Constr.Bn., 246 Constr.Bn.,

4th, 7th, 48th AA Regt.

XXXXII CORPS

39th, 161st, 282nd Inf. Div.

Corps Troops

FIELD ARTILLERY

Arko 107, 2nd/800th 15cm Gun Bty., 13th Art.Obsv.Bn.

OTHERS

620th Mtn.Eng.Regt. (m), 26th Constr. Regt., 219th, 112th Constr. Bn. (U), 153rd Constr. Bn. (K), AT Bn. C., 560th Hvy. AT Bn. (Nashorn), 18th Penal Bn.

Army Troops

Higher Arko 310, Commander of Smoketroops 1, 781st Art. Regt. Staff, 22nd Constr. Bde., 21st Bridge Constr. Bn., 538th, 676th Hvy.Road Constr. Bn.

9TH ARMY, 30 JUNE

XX CORPS

45th, 72nd, 137th, 251st Inf. Div.

Corps Troops

FIELD ARTILLERY

Arko 129, 860th Field Art.Bn., 15th Lt.Art.Obsv.Bn.

ENGINEERS

512th Eng.Regt.Staff, 4th Eng.Regt. staff, 750th Eng.Bn., Bridge Column B 626, 44th, 418th, 80th Constr.Bn., 244th Constr.Bn. (K)

XXXXVI PANZER CORPS

7th, 31st, 102nd, 258th Inf. Div.

Corps Troops

FIELD ARTILLERY

Arko 1, 609th Art.Regt.Staff, 909th Assault Gun Bn., 430th Field Art.Bn., 611th 10cm Gun Bn., II/47th Mixed Art.Bn., 3rd/637th 21cm How.Bty., 3rd/620th 15cm Gun Bty., 1st Recoilless Gun Bn. (with 423, 433 and 443 Bty.), 18th Hvy.Mtr.Bn.

OTHERS

752nd Eng.Bn., Bridge Column B 12, 29, Bridging Staff 930, Commander of Constr.Forces 33, 584th Road Constr.Bn., Group von Manteuffel (9th, 10th, 11th Jaeger Bn.)

XXXXVII PANZER CORPS

6th Inf. Div., 2nd, 9th, 20th Pz. Div.

Corps Troops

FIELD ARTILLERY

Arko 130, 904th, 245th Assault Gun Bn., II/63rd, II/67th Hvy.Field Bn., 637th 21cm How.Bn. (minus 3rd Bty.), 1st/620th 15cm Gun Bty, 2nd Hvy.Rocket-Launcher Regt

OTHERS

678th Eng.Regt.Staff, 2nd Training Eng.Bn., 47th Eng.Bn. (m), 145th

Bridge Constr.Bn., Bridging Staff 928, 505th Hvy.Tank Bn. (minus 3rd Coy.), 312th Pz. Coy. (Fkl)

XXXXI PANZER CORPS

86th, 292nd Inf. Div. and 18th Pz. Div.

Corps Troops

FIELD ARTILLERY

Arko 35, 69th Art.Regt.Staff, 177th, 244th Assault Gun Bn., 616th, 425th, II/64th Field Art.Bn., 427th 10cm Gun Bn., II/61st Hvy.Field Art.Bn., 604th 21cm How.Bn., 2nd/620th 15cm Gun Bty., 53rd Rocket Art.Regt., 19th Hvy.Mtr.Bn.

OTHERS

104th Eng.Regt.Staff, 42nd Eng.Bn. (m), Bridging Staff 932 (Bridge Column B 2/409, 606), 407th Constr. Bn., 656th Tank Destroyer Regt.

XXIII CORPS

216th, 383rd Inf. Div., 87th Gren Regt (from 36th ID) and 78th Assault Div.

Corps Troops

FIELD ARTILLERY

Arko 112, 109th, 41st, 774th Art. Regt. Staff, 185th, 189th Assault Gun Bn., II/59th, 426th, 851st Field Art.Bn., 79th 10cm Gun Bn., 4th/69th 10cm Gun Bty., 422nd Mixed Art.Bn., 848th, II/66th Hvy.Field Art.Bn., 859th, 1st, 2nd/635th 21cm How.Bty., 1st/817th 17cm Gun Bty., 22nd Lt.Art.Obsv.Bn., 51st Rocket Art. Regt.

OTHERS

623rd Eng.Regt.Staff, 746th Eng.Bn., 85th Mtn.Eng.Bn., Bridge Column B 88, 78th Road Constr.Bn., 811th, 813th Armd Eng.Coy., 8th, 13th Jaeger Bn.

Army Troops

442nd Div. Staff, Cmndr of Smoke Troops 4, 654th Eng.Bn., 751st Eng.Bn., 42nd, 539th Bridge Constr.Bn., Bridge Column B 1/430th, 535th, Cmdr of Constr. Forces 42, 544th, 576th, 580th Road Constr.Bn., Higher Constr.Staff 10, 889th Sec.Bn.

ARMY GROUP CENTRE RESERVE

4th, 12th Pz. Div., 10th Pz. Gren Div.

LUFTWAFFE, 4 JULY

VIIITH AIR CORPS (Luftflotte 4) supporting Army Group South.
1ST AIR DIVISION (Luftflotte 6) supporting Army Group Centre.